STRIPTEASE, TANGO, VATZLAV

Three Plays By
Slawomir Mrozek

Grove Press, Inc.   New York

D0862113

This collection copyright © 1981 by Grove Press, Inc.

Striptease copyright © 1972 by Slawomir Mrozek.
English translation copyright 1972 by Grove Press, Inc.
Tango copyright © 1968 by Slawomir Mrozek.
English translation copyright © 1968 by Grove Press, Inc.
Vatzlav copyright © 1970 by Slawomir Mrozek.
English version copyright © 1970 by Grove Press, Inc.

Library of Congress Cataloging in Publication Data

Mrozek, Slawomir.
    Striptease; Tango; Vatzlav: three plays.
    Selected plays, translated from the Polish.

    I. Title.
PG7172.R65   1981   891.8'527   81-47635
ISBN 0-394-17933-1 (pbk.)   AACR2

First Evergreen Edition 1981
First Printing 1981
ISBN: 0-394-17933-1
Library of Congress Catalog Card Number: 81-47635

Manufactured in the United States of America

GROVE PRESS, INC., 196 West Houston Street, New York, N.Y. 10014

STRIPTEASE

Translated by Lola Gruenthal

Cast of Characters

MR. I

MR. II

The stage is bare except for two chairs. Two doors, one stage left and one stage right, should be in clear view of the audience. When the curtain rises there is no one on stage. One can hear strange rattling and rumbling noises which may sound vaguely familiar but cannot be identified. The door on stage left opens and MR. I *comes rushing in. He is middle-aged, neatly but conventionally dressed, and carries a briefcase. Obviously he is not interested in his present environment but is rather preoccupied with something that has just happened outside. He should convey the impression that he has not entered the stage of his own will. He finally looks around and adjusts his suit. The door remains slightly ajar. A few moments later* MR. II *rushes in through the door on stage right. He looks like an exact replica of* MR. I *and also carries a briefcase. The second door is not completely closed either.*

MR. I: Extraordinary!

MR. II: Incredible!

MR. I: I was walking along as usual . . .

MR. II: Not a care in the world . . .

MR. I: When suddenly . . .

MR. II: Like a bolt from the sky . . .

MR. I (*as though just becoming aware of the presence of* MR. II): How did you get here?

MR. II: Why don't you ask what brought me here, or who brought me here?

MR. I (*again following his own thoughts*): Outrageous!

MR. II (*as though slightly mimicking* MR. I): Preposterous!

MR. I: I was simply walking, or perhaps, rather, hurrying along . . .

MR. II: Yes, that's right! You were certainly heading for a particular destination.

MR. I: How do you know?

MR. II: It's obvious. I was walking along too, or rather, hurrying along, heading for my destination.

MR. I: You took the words right out of my mouth. As I said, I was heading for this destination when suddenly . . .

MR. II: And remember, this was a destination that you yourself had chosen.

MR. I: Exactly! And with conscious intent, mind you, with full conscious intent . . .

MR. II: Obeying the dictates of your conscience, motivated by faith and reason.

MR. I: You're reading my very thoughts. As I was saying, I followed the path most appropriate for my chosen destination when suddenly . . .

MR. II (*confidentially*): They beat you?

MR. I: Oh, no! (*Also confidentially.*) And you?

MR. II: God forbid! I mean, I don't know a thing. That's all I can say.

MR. I: What was it then?

MR. II: That's hard to say for sure. It was like a gigantic elephant blocking the street. Or were there riots? First I had the impression of a flood, then of a picnic. But being in such a fog . . .

MR. I: That's true! It's so foggy today you can hardly see a thing. Still, I was trying to reach my particular destination . . .

MR. II: Which you yourself had freely chosen . . .

MR. I: That's God's honest truth! Nothing was left to chance. I had prepared everything down to the last detail. My wife and I often spend long hours planning ahead, planning our entire lives.

MR. II: I also had it all mapped out in advance. Even as a child . . .

MR. I (*confidentially*): Did you hear a voice?

MR. II: I certainly did. There was a voice.

MR. I: Something like a saw . . . a persistent sound . . . no, actually an intermittent one.

MR. II: A gigantic buzz saw.

MR. I: But where the hell could a saw come from?

MR. II: Perhaps it wasn't a saw. Something threw me to the ground.

MR. I: But what?

MR. II: The worst part is this uncertainty. Was it really to the ground?

MR. I: Where else if not to the ground?

MR. II: But was I really thrown? What a jungle of riddles! I can't even tell if this was a "being-thrown" in the exact, classical sense, deserving of the name. Though I had the sensation of being thrown down, lying on the ground, I was perhaps——

MR. I (*tensely*): More overthrown than thrown down?

MR. II: Precisely! And to tell the truth, I really have no complaints. Did you see any people?

MR. I: Are there any at all?

MR. II: I suppose there are, but with all this fog . . . it doesn't seem likely.

MR. I: The worst of all is this lack of assurance.

MR. II: What color was it?

MR. I: What?

MR. II: It's so hard to figure out anything. It was something bright . . . a sort of rose color shot through with lead.

MR. I: Nonsense!

MR. II (*moving over to* MR. I, *after a pause*): And still they hit you in the jaw.

MR. I: Me?

MR. II: Me too.

Pause.

MR. I: Well, anyway, now I can't get there on time anymore.

MR. II: How about just walking out? Right now! As though nothing had happened?

MR. I: No, no!

MR. II: Are you afraid?

MR. I: Me? Why should I be? I'm just a little nervous. I just can't see . . .

MR. II: That's because of the fog.

MR. I: Did they say we must not leave the room?

MR. II: Who?

MR. I: Whom were you thinking of?

MR. II: Never mind!

MR. I: I've decided to stay put. The situation will clear up by itself.

MR. II: But why? It may be quite possible for us to leave this room, unimpeded, and to continue on our way. After all, we can't really tell what's going on. Perhaps we ourselves went astray.

MR. I: Are you blaming yourself? Us? We both knew where we were going, each of us heading for his specific destination.

MR. II: Then it was not our own fault?

MR. I: No, unless . . .

MR. II: Unless?

MR. I: How do I know? Let's drop the subject! I, for one, feel most strongly that we should not leave this room.

MR. II: If you're so sure about it . . .

MR. I: Definitely! We have to use sound reasoning in dealing with this matter.

Both sit down.

MR. II: Perhaps you're right. (*Listens.*) There's nobody there.

MR. I: Actually, there's no cause for concern, is there?

MR. II: No obvious cause, I would say.

MR. I: Are you implying that there is a cause . . . an obscure one?

MR. II: You have a mind of your own.

MR. I: Let's establish the facts.

MR. II: All right, go ahead.

MR. I: Very well, then: Each of us left his house according to plan and walked, or rather hurried, as you observed correctly, in the direction of his goal. The morning was brisk, the weather fair, the existence of wife and children an established fact. Each of us knew whatever there was to be known. Of course, we had no exact idea about the kind of molecules, not to speak of atoms, that our bedside tables are composed of, but, after all, there are specialists who deal with such matters. Basically, everything was perfectly clear. Wellshaved, carrying our practical and indispensable briefcases, we set out purposefully toward our goal. The respective addresses had been thoroughly committed to memory. But to be quite safe we had also noted them down in our notebooks. Am I correct?

MR. II: On every point.

MR. I: Now listen carefully! At a certain moment, as we were pursuing our course, a course that we had mapped out in detail and that was, so to speak, the end result of all our rational calculations, something happened which . . . and this is a point I must stress . . . came entirely from the outside, something separate in itself and independent of us.

MR. II: With regard to this point, I must register some doubt. Since we are unable to define the exact nature of the occurrence, and since we cannot even agree as to its manifestations . . . due to the fog or to whatever other causes . . . we are in no position to state with any degree of certainty that this something came exclusively from the outside or that it was entirely separate in itself and independent of us.

MR. I: You are discomposing me.

MR. II: I beg your pardon?

MR. I: You're interrupting my thoughts.

MR. II: I'm sorry.

MR. I: Unfortunately, we are not able to determine the exact nature of the phenomenon, and . . .

MR. II: That's just what I said.

MR. I: If you wish to go on, don't mind me!

MR. II: The words just slipped out. It won't happen again.

MR. I (*continuing*): We cannot even determine with any appropriate degree of accuracy what particular elements constituted this something. (*Pause.*) I beg your pardon?

MR. II: I didn't say a thing.

MR. I: I, for instance, perceived something that seemed to have the shape of an animal, but still I cannot be absolutely sure that it was not at the same time a mineral. Actually, it seems to me that it involved energy rather than matter. I think all this may be best defined as a phenomenon hovering on the borderline of dimensions and definitions, a connecting link between color, form, smell, weight, length, and breadth, shade, light, dark, and so on and so forth.

MR. II: Do you still feel any pain? Mine is almost all gone.

MR. I: Please don't reduce everything to its lowest level!

MR. II: I was just asking.

MR. I (*continuing his train of thought*): This much is certain: We were helpless in the face of the phenomenon, and, partly of our own will, as we were looking for shelter, partly due to external pressure, we happened to find ourselves in these strange quarters which at that critical moment were close at hand. Fortunately, we found the doors open. Needless to say, our original intentions have thus been completely upset and, as it were, arrested.

MR. II: I fully agree. What are your conclusions?

MR. I: This is just what I was coming to. Our main task now is to preserve our calm and our personal dignity. Thus, it would seem to me, we still remain in control of the situation. Basically, our freedom is in no way limited.

MR. II: You call this freedom, our sitting here?

MR. I: But we can walk out at any moment . . . the doors are open.

MR. II: Then let's go! We've wasted too much time anyway.

Again the same strange noise is heard as in the beginning.

MR. I: What . . . ? What's that?

MR. II: I told you we should go.

MR. I: Right now?

MR. II: Are you afraid?

MR. I: Not at all.

MR. II: First you insist on preserving your personal dignity by asserting your freedom, and then you don't even want to leave while there is still time.

MR. I: If I left right now I would limit the idea of freedom.

MR. II: What do you mean?

MR. I: It's quite obvious. What is freedom? It is the capacity of making a choice. As long as I am sitting here, knowing that I can walk out of this door, I am free. But as soon as I get up and walk out, I have already made my choice, I have limited the possible courses of action, I have lost my freedom. I become the slave of my own locomotion.

MR. II: But your sitting here and not walking out is just another way of making a choice. You simply choose sitting rather than leaving.

MR. I: Wrong! While I'm sitting, I can still leave. If, however, I do leave, I preclude the alternative of sitting.

MR. II: And this makes you feel comfortable?

MR. I: Perfectly comfortable. Unlimited inner freedom, that is my answer to these strange happenings. (MR. II *gets up.*) What are you doing?

MR. II: I'm leaving. I don't like this.

MR. I: Are you joking?

MR. II: I'm not trying to. I believe in external freedom.

MR. I: And what about me?

MR. II: Goodbye.

MR. I: Please wait! Are you crazy? You don't even know what's out there!

Both doors close slowly.

MR. II: Hey! What's going on now?

MR. I: Don't close them! Don't close them!

MR. II: All because of your babbling! We should have made up our minds right away.

MR. I: You don't have to blame me. If you had sat still, the doors wouldn't have closed. It was your fault.

MR. II: Now there's no way of finding out.

MR. I: It's all because of you. Thanks to your behavior we've lost our chance to get out.

MR. II *goes to one of the doors and tries unsuccessfully to open it.*

MR. II: Hey! Open up right now!

MR. I: Shh! Be quiet!

MR. II: Why should I be quiet?

MR. I: I don't know.

MR. II (*goes to the other door, knocks, and listens*): Locked!

MR. I: Do me a favor and sit down!

MR. II: Well, where is it now, your precious freedom?

MR. I: I have nothing to blame myself for. My freedom remains unaffected.

MR. II: But there's no way to get out now, is there?

MR. I: The potential of my freedom has remained unchanged. I have not made a choice, I have in no way confined myself. The doors were closed for external reasons. I am the same person that I was before. As you may have noticed, I did not even get up from my chair.

MR. II: These doors are upsetting me.

MR. I: My dear sir, while we are unable to influence external events, we must make every effort to preserve our dignity and our inner balance. And with regard to those, we command an unlimited field, even though the infinite variety of choices has been reduced to two alternatives. These, of course, exist only as long as we do not choose either of them.

MR. II: What else could happen?

MR. I: Do you think it may get worse?

MR. II: I'll try to knock on the wall . . . perhaps somebody is there.

MR. I: It is regrettable that you have no regard for the inviolable nature of your personal freedom. I, too, could knock on the wall, but I won't. If I did, I would preclude other possibilities, such as reading the papers I have in my briefcase or concentrating on last year's horse races.

MR. II *knocks on the wall several times and listens; he repeats this for a while. Then he takes off one shoe and bangs with it against the wall. One of the doors opens slowly, and in comes a Hand of supernatural size. It resembles the old-fashioned printer's symbol: Hand with pointing index finger and attached cuff. The palm should be brightly colored to make it stand out clearly against the scenery. With bent index finger the Hand makes a monotonously repeated gesture in the direction of* MR. II, *beckoning to him.*

MR. I (*the first to notice the Hand*): Pssst! (MR. II *has not yet seen the Hand; he keeps banging with his shoe and listening.*) Pssst! Stop it, please! Don't you see what's going on?

MR. II *turns around.* MR. I *points to the Hand.*

MR. II: Something new again!

The Hand continues beckoning to him. MR. II *walks over to it. The Hand points to the shoe he is holding, then it reaches out in an ambiguous gesture that may be either begging or demanding. Hesitantly,* MR. II *puts his shoe into the Hand. The Hand disappears and returns immediately without the shoe.* MR. II *takes off his other shoe and gives it to the Hand. The Hand leaves the room, returns, and repeatedly touches* MR. II's *stomach with its index finger. Guessing what this means,* MR. II *takes off his belt and hands it over. The Hand withdraws, returns without the belt, and begins to beckon to* MR. I.

MR. I: Me? (*He slowly walks over to the Hand, stopping at every other step. While he is talking, the Hand continually beckons to him.*) But I didn't knock ... There must be a misunderstanding ... I didn't make a choice ... no choice whatsoever ... I did not knock, though I must admit that when my colleague knocked I was hoping that someone might hear it and come in, that the situation might be cleared up and that we would be allowed to leave. This much I admit, but I didn't do any knocking. (*The Hand points to his shoes.*) I protest. I repeat once more: The knocking was not done by me. I don't understand why I should hand over my shoes. (*Bends down to untie the laces.*) I value my inner freedom. A little patience, please! Can't the Hand see that there's a knot here? ... Personally, I don't hold anything against the Hand, because my own conscience is clear. I am determined to save my inner freedom, even at the cost of my external freedom ... quite the opposite to my colleague here. But I'm not holding anything against him either, because, after all, what he does is his own business. I request only that we be treated as individuals, each according to his own views ... Just a moment, I'm getting it. There's no fire, is there? (*Giving the Hand his shoes.*) Glad to oblige! (*The Hand points to his stomach.*) I'm not wearing a belt ... I prefer suspenders. All right, I'll give up the suspenders, too, if necessary. (*Takes off his jacket and unbuttons his suspenders.*) Peculiar methods they have here! All right, here they are ... Somebody's fingernails could use a good cleaning, if I may venture an opinion. (*The Hand disappears, the door closes slowly.*) At least I'm wearing a fresh pair of socks. I'm glad about that.

MR. II: Boot licker!

MR. I: Leave me alone! I'm not bothering you.

MR. II: What can I use now to knock with?

MR. I: That's your problem. I'm going to sit down. (*Returns to his chair.*)

MR. II: You're in good shape now with your inner freedom. You're losing your pants.

MR. I: What about yours? They won't stay up either without a belt.

MR. II: Well, what do you make of all this?

MR. I: I can only repeat what I said before: First the dear Hand interfered with my free movement in space and then with my ability to wear trousers. This is true, and this I'm willing to admit. But what does it matter? All these are externals. Inwardly I have remained free. I have not become engaged in any action, I have not made any gesture. I haven't even moved a finger. Just sitting here I am still free to do whatever lies in the realm of possibility. Not you, though. You did some-

thing . . . you made a choice . . . you knocked against
the wall and made a fool of yourself. Slave!

MR. II: I could slap your face, but there are more important
things to be done.

MR. I: Right. But why do they deal with us like this?

MR. II: It's always the first thing they do . . . take away
your shoe laces, belts, and suspenders.

MR. I: What for?

MR. II: So you can't hang yourself.

MR. I: You must be joking! If I'm not even getting up from
my chair, how can I hang myself? Of course, I could if
I wanted to, but I won't. You know my views.

MR. II: I'm sick and tired of your views.

MR. I: That's your problem. But listen to this: If the dear
Hand doesn't want us to hang ourselves, this means
that it wants to keep us alive. That's a good sign!

MR. II: This is just what bothers me. It means that the
Hand thinks of us in terms of categories . . . Life and
the other . . . what's it called?

MR. I: Death?

MR. II: You said it.

Pause.

MR. I: I am calm.

MR. II: Tell me, what could you do now, if you felt like doing something? Of course, taking into account the fact
that you had to relinquish your shoes and suspenders.

MR. I: Oh, quite a few things. I could, for instance, put on
my jacket inside out, roll up the legs of my trousers,
and pretend to be a fisherman.

MR. II: And what else?

MR. I: I could sing.

MR. II: That's enough. (*Turns up the legs of his trousers, puts on his jacket inside out, and takes off his socks.*)

MR. I: Are you crazy? What are you trying to do?

MR. II: I'm pretending to be a fisherman, and I'm going to sing, too. In contrast to you, I want to explore all the possibilities of action. Maybe the Hand is partial to fishermen and lets them return to freedom. Who knows? One should not neglect any possibility. I've asked you because you have more imagination than I. For instance, I could never have thought up all those things about inner freedom.

MR. I: It's all right with me. But please remember that I'm not moving from this chair.

MR. II: You don't have to. (*He climbs on the chair and sings Schubert's "The Trout." One of the doors slowly opens.*)

MR. I (*who has been anxiously watching the door*): Now you've done it!

The Hand appears.

MR. II: How do you know? Perhaps I'll be allowed to go and you'll keep sitting. (*The Hand beckons to him.*) I'm coming, I'm coming. What's it all about? (*The Hand indicates that it wants his jacket.*) But I was just—— Is there a law against fishing? (*The Hand repeats its gesture.*) I was just pretending. I'm not really a fisherman. (*Gives the Hand his jacket. The Hand disappears, comes back, and now obviously requests his trousers.*) No, I won't give up the trousers! (*The Hand forms a fist and slowly rises.*) All right. (*He takes off his trousers.*)

MR. I (*getting up*): Me too?

After waiting for an answer, which he does not receive, MR. I voluntarily removes his jacket. Meanwhile MR. II has given the Hand his trousers, and he now stands there in striped knee-length underpants. The Hand carries the trousers backstage, returns immediately and beckons to MR. I.

MR. I: All right, here it is. I'm not resisting, and I beg the Hand to take this into consideration. (*He gives his jacket to the Hand, which takes it out and returns immediately.*) I'm always willing to oblige . . . may I keep my trousers in return? (*The Hand makes a negative gesture.*) All right, I won't protest.

He takes off his trousers and stands up in his underpants, identical to those of MR. II. The Hand disappears, the door closes.

MR. I: You can go to hell with your idea about fishermen.

MR. II: It seems to me that it was your idea.

MR. I: But you carried it out. It's cold in here.

MR. II: It's quite possible that we might have been ordered to hand over our clothes anyway, idea or no idea.

MR. I: No! I'm convinced it was you who got us both into this predicament with your idiotic masquerade. It was you who attracted the Hand's attention to our clothing. If at least you had not rolled up your trousers, they would not have caught its eye.

MR. II: But fishermen always roll up their trousers.

MR. I: What good does that do you now?

MR. II: You can't keep ignoring the fact that we differ in our views. You do nothing so that you can feel free to do anything—of course, within the range of what is permitted—while I try to do everything I am permitted to do. But apparently wearing trousers is not permitted.

MR. I: You yourself have brought this down on your head.

MR. II: An anatomical inaccuracy! Besides, let me repeat this once more: We don't know whether the removal of our clothes was provoked by my action or whether it was part of a predetermined plan.

MR. I: At least now you should realize that my basic attitude is superior to yours. Don't you see: I didn't knock, I didn't sing, I didn't roll up my trousers, and still, here I am, looking just like you. Even our stripes are the same.

MR. II: Where is your superiority then?

MR. I: No waste of energy; same results. Plus, of course, my sense of inner freedom which . . .

MR. II: One more word about inner freedom and that will be the end of you.

MR. I (*backing up*): You're unfair! After all, everyone has a right to choose the philosophy that suits him best.

MR. II: Never mind! I can't stand this anymore!

MR. I: I'm warning you: I won't defend myself. Defending oneself involves making a choice, and for me this is out, in the name of . . .

MR. II: What? Go on! In the name of what?

MR. I (*hesitantly*): In the name of inner free—— (MR. II

throws himself at him. MR. I *runs all over the stage.)*
Keep your hands off!

*The door opens and the Hand reappears, beckoning to
both.* MR. I *and* MR. II *come to a sudden halt.*

MR. II: Me?
MR. I: Or me?
MR. II: Maybe it's you . . .
MR. I: You started this fight. Now you'll get your just de-
serts.
MR. II: Why me? Do you still believe that your idiotic
theory is better?
MR. I: And you believe that your vulgar pragmatism, this
lack of any theory, will stand up to such a test?

The Hand beckons to both.

MR. II: We'd better go over! It wants something again.
MR. I: All right, let's go! We'll soon find out who is right.

*They go over to the Hand which links them together
with a pair of handcuffs. The Hand disappears and the
door closes.* MR. II *drags* MR. I *along with him by the
chain of the handcuffs and collapses on his chair.
Silence.*

MR. I: What does this mean? (*Anxiously.*) Aren't you feel-
ing well? Do you believe that this time it's serious?
Say something, please!
MR. II: I'm afraid . . .
MR. I: Of what?
MR. II: So far the Hand has limited only our freedom of
movement in space. But what assurance is there that

soon we won't be limited in something even more essential?

MR. I: In what?

MR. II: In time. In our own duration.

Pause.

MR. I: I don't know either. (*Pedantically.*) You, of course, being an activist, will exhaust your energies more rapidly. I, on the other hand, conserve mine . . .

MR. II (*imploringly*): Not again!

MR. I: I'm sorry. I didn't mean to hurt your feelings. Do you have a plan?

MR. II: There is only one thing we can do now.

MR. I: What?

MR. II: Apologize to the Hand.

MR. I: Apologize? But what for? We haven't done anything to the Hand. On the contrary, it should . . .

MR. II: This is completely irrelevant. We have to apologize all the same . . . in general, for no reason. To save ourselves . . . for whatever good it may do.

MR. I: No, I can't do that. I don't suppose I have to explain my reasons.

MR. II: You're right, I know them by heart. To apologize to the Hand would mean to make a choice, which again would limit your freedom, and so on and so forth.

MR. I: Yes, that's how it is.

MR. II: Do as you please! In any case, I am going to apologize. One has to abase oneself. Perhaps that is what it expects us to do.

MR. I: I would like to join you, but my principles . . .

MR. II: I have nothing more to say.

MR. I: I think I can see a way out. You're going to force me to apologize with you. In that case there is no question of choice on my part. I'm simply going to be forced.

MR. II: All right, consider yourself forced.

The door opens.

MR. I: I think it's coming. (*The Hand appears.*) If only we had some flowers! (*Whispering.*) You start!

Both run over to the Hand. MR. II *clears his throat in preparation for his apology.*

MR. II: Dear Hand! I mean, Dear and Most Honorable Hand! Although well aware of the fact that the Hand is not here to listen to us, we still beg permission to speak to the Hand from the heart... I mean, we would like to hand the Hand a confession, although somewhat belated, nevertheless with full conscious awareness, we sincerely beg to apologize for... for... (*Whispering to* MR. I.) For what?

MR. I: For walking, for going ahead, for everything in general...

MR. II: For walking, for going ahead, for... I'm expressing myself poorly, but I simply wish to apologize in general... for having been... for being... begging forgiveness from the depth of my heart for whatever the Honorable Hand knows that we don't know... for how are we to know what there is to be known? Therefore, whatever the case may be, I humbly apologize, I beg the Hand's forgiveness, I kiss the Hand. (*He ceremoniously kisses the Hand.*)

MR. I: I wish to join my colleague, though only in a certain sense, having been forced ... The Hand knows my principles ... Therefore, though being forced, I nevertheless sincerely apologize to the Hand on principle.

He ceremoniously kisses the Hand. Meanwhile the other door opens and through it appears a Second Hand, completely covered by a red glove. It beckons to both. MR. II notices it first. Both turn their backs to the First Hand.

MR. II: There! Look!
MR. I: Another one!
MR. II: There are always two.
MR. I: It's calling us.
MR. II: Should we go? (*The First Hand covers his head with a conical cardboard hood.*) I can't see anything!
MR. I: It's calling us. (*The First Hand covers his head with an identical hood.*) It's dark.
MR. II: When you're called, you have to go.

Handcuffed to each other and blinded by the hoods, they move toward stage center. Constantly stumbling and swerving, they gradually come closer to the Second Hand.

MR. I: The briefcases! We forgot our briefcases!
MR. II: Right! My briefcase! Where's my briefcase?

They grope blindly for their briefcases, left standing next to the chairs, then pick them up and follow the Second Hand through the door. Blackout.

TANGO

A Play in Three Acts

Translated by Ralph Manheim and Teresa Dzieduscycka

Tango was first performed at the Jugoslovensko Dramsko Pozoriske in Belgrade, Yugoslavia on April 21, 1965. The first Polish performance took place in Warsaw on July 7, 1965 at the Teatr Wspòłozesny, directed by Erwin Axer. The first performance of *Tango* in New York took place at the Pocket Theater on January 20, 1969. The production was staged by Heinz Engels and based on the original staging by Erwin Axer, with setting by Jason Phillips, costumes by John E. Hirsch, lighting by Paul Holland, and dance arranged by Jon Devlin. The cast was as follows:

EUGENIA	Muriel Kirkland
EDDIE	Clifford A. Pellow
EUGENE	Arthur Ed Forman
ARTHUR	David Margulies
ELEANOR	Lilyan Wilder
STOMIL	Stefan Schnabel
ALA	Elizabeth Swain

Photographs of the New York production by Arthur Cantor

ACT ONE

A large, high room. The wall on the right ("right" and "left" are always taken from the point of view of the audience) is not visible. This gives the impression that the room extends beyond the edge of the stage. The wall on the left does not reach to the front of the stage but forms a right angle a few steps behind it and continues leftward along the proscenium. Between this corner of the wall and the left edge of the stage there is a door leading into a second room. This produces a kind of corridor leading off-stage to the left and into the main room on the right. At the left and right of the rear wall, two more doors. The doors all look the same: double doors, high, painted a dark color, and ornamented in a style befitting old, solidly middle-class houses. Between the two doors in the rear wall, an alcove covered by a curtain. In the room: a table with eight chairs, armchairs, a couch, small tables, a large mirror on the left-hand wall. The furniture is arranged haphazardly as though the family had just moved in or were about to move out. Great confusion. In addition, the whole stage is full of draperies, hanging, lying or rolled, adding to the impression of confusion and blurring the outlines of the room. The room seems to be covered with spots. At one point on the floor draperies are thrown into a heap, forming a kind of bed. An old-fashioned black baby carriage on high, thin wheels. A dusty wedding dress. A derby hat. The velvet tablecloth is shoved half-aside. Three persons are seated at the uncovered part of the table. The first, who will be called

GRANDMA for the present, is an elderly but well-preserved and lively lady, who suffers only occasionally from senile absentmindedness. Her dress, in a garish-colored flower pattern, has a train attached; she wears a jockey cap and sneakers. She seems to be near-sighted. A gray-haired, extremely polite old man. He is wearing glasses with thin gold rims, but his dress is disordered, and he seems dusty and intimidated. Swallow-tail coat, dirty stiff collar, a wide tie with a pearl stickpin, but khaki-colored shorts, scotch-plaid knee socks, torn patent-leather shoes, bare knees. The third individual, who gives the impression of being crude and shady, wears baggy, light-gray, rumpled pants and an ugly checked shirt, open at the chest. His shirtsleeves are rolled up. He habitually scratches his fat behind. Long greasy hair, which he frequently combs with a comb which he takes from his back pocket. Small, square mustache. Unshaven. A watch with a shiny gold wristband. All three are deep in their card game. On the velvet tablecloth: dishes, cups, carafes, artificial flowers, scraps of food. But also a few incongruous objects: a large, empty, bottomless bird cage; a lady's shoe; a pair of riding breeches. Even more than the rest of the furnishings, this table gives an impression of haphazardness, eccentricity and disorder. Each plate comes from a different set, each object is of a different period and style. From the right enters a young man of twenty-five at the most: imposing and pleasant appearance. Neat, freshly pressed, ready-made suit that fits him perfectly, white shirt, tie. Under his arm he is carrying books and papers. He stands still and observes the scene. The three card players do not notice him. The table is quite far to the left. The person temporarily known as GRANDMA is sitting with her back to the young man, her profile to the audience. The elderly gentleman is facing her. At the head of

*the table the third player, with his back to the audience.
The young man who has just come in is to one side of him.*

PERSON TEMPORARILY KNOWN AS GRANDMA (*throwing a card
on the table with exaggerated gusto*): Three of spades.
Razor blades.

PLAYER WITH MUSTACHE (*throwing down a card*): Down
on the table goes old Aunt Mabel. (*He drinks beer
from a bottle standing beside his chair.*)

OLD GENTLEMAN (*timidly clearing his throat; speaks with a
visible effort*): Indeed, yes. I mean. . . . Well, plunk!
(*He throws down a card.*)

PERSON TEMPORARILY KNOWN AS GRANDMA (*waits for a moment, then with disapproval*): Plunk! Oh come on,
Eugene! Plunk what?

OLD GENTLEMAN *or* EUGENE (*stuttering helplessly*): Plunk
. . . plunk. . . .

PLAYER WITH MUSTACHE: The old gentleman's not in form
today.

He takes a swig from the bottle.

PERSON TEMPORARILY KNOWN AS GRANDMA: Eugene! If
you're going to play with us, you've got to do it right.
Plunk's all right, but then what?

EUGENE: Well, just plain plunk!

PERSON TEMPORARILY KNOWN AS GRANDMA: Good Lord,
you're blushing again!

EUGENE: Well then, plunk—trunk. Will that do?

PERSON TEMPORARILY KNOWN AS GRANDMA: Certainly not.
Why don't you help him out, Eddie?

PLAYER WITH MUSTACHE *or* EDDIE: ith plunk? That's a
tough word to work with. How about: Scram, Sam.
We're on the lam.

EUGENE: Splendid! Splendid. But if you'll excuse my asking, what does it mean? Who's on the lam?

EDDIE: It's what they say, that's all.

PERSON TEMPORARILY KNOWN AS GRANDMA: Eugene. Eddie knows best.

EUGENE (*throwing the same card on the table again*): Scram, Sam. We're on the lam.

PERSON TEMPORARILY KNOWN AS GRANDMA: See, with a little effort you can do it too.

EDDIE: The old gentleman is a bit bashful.

PERSON TEMPORARILY KNOWN AS GRANDMA: Thank you, Eddie dear. I don't know what we would do without you.

EDDIE: Don't mention it. (*He sees the* YOUNG MAN *and quickly hides the bottle under the table.*) I'd better be leaving.

PERSON TEMPORARILY KNOWN AS GRANDMA: What? Why? What's got into you? Right in the middle of our game?

YOUNG MAN: Good morning!

PERSON TEMPORARILY KNOWN AS GRANDMA (*turns around, annoyed*): Oh, it's you.

YOUNG MAN: Yes, me. What's going on here anyway?

PERSON TEMPORARILY KNOWN AS GRANDMA: What do you mean? We're just having our little game.

YOUNG MAN: I can see that. But with whom?

PERSON TEMPORARILY KNOWN AS GRANDMA: With whom? Don't you recognize your Uncle Eugene any more?

YOUNG MAN: I wasn't asking about Uncle Eugene. I'll settle with him later. Who is this individual? (*He indicates* EDDIE.)

EDDIE (*stands up*): I'll just be running along now: Madam, the pleasure was mine.

PERSON TEMPORARILY KNOWN AS GRANDMA: Edward! Stay!

YOUNG MAN: Out! Out!

EDDIE (*reproachfully to* GRANDMA): Dear lady, didn't I tell you we shouldn't have played today?

EUGENE (*pointing to* GRANDMA): It's her fault. Entirely her fault. I didn't even want to play.

YOUNG MAN (*stepping up to the table*): I said Out!

EDDIE: Easy, Aces. I'm going!

On his way out he comes close to the YOUNG MAN. *He takes one of the books from under his arm and opens it.*

YOUNG MAN (*rushing toward the table*): How often have I told you never to let this happen again?

He runs around the table in pursuit of GRANDMA, *who tries to evade him.*

PERSON TEMPORARILY KNOWN AS GRANDMA: No! No!

YOUNG MAN: Oh yes, oh yes! And right now too!

EDDIE (*leafing through the book*): Fabulous!

PERSON TEMPORARILY KNOWN AS GRANDMA: What do you want of me anyway?

YOUNG MAN (*running after her*): You know very well what I want.

EUGENE: Arthur, have you no pity for your own grandmother?

YOUNG MAN, *or* ARTHUR: Oh, so you're talking back again are you, Uncle?

EUGENE: Not at all. I simply wanted to say that even if Eugenia may have forgotten herself a bit . . .

ARTHUR: Then I'll just have to remind her. And you too, Uncle. Pity! How can you talk about pity? Do any of you have any pity for me? Does she ever try to understand me? Oh, but this time, Uncle, you're going to get what's coming to you. Why aren't you working? Why aren't you writing your memoirs?

EUGENE: I did write a bit this morning, but then they came barging into my room, and . . .

PERSON HITHERTO KNOWN AS GRANDMA, *or* EUGENIA: Eugene! Traitor!

EUGENE (*hysterically*): Why can't you all just leave me in peace?

ARTHUR: Oh, we will. But you've got to be punished too. (*He puts the bottomless bird cage over Eugene's head.*) Now sit there until I let you out.

EUGENIA: Serves him right.

ARTHUR: Don't think you're going to get off free. (*He pulls back the curtain over the alcove, revealing a catafalque covered with a discolored black cloth and surmounted by several candelabra.*) Hup! Up you go!

EDDIE (*looking through the book with increasing interest*): Terrific! (*He sits down off to one side.*)

EUGENIA: Again? I don't want to!

ARTHUR: Not another word!

EUGENIA *humbly approaches the catafalque,* EUGENE *attentively offers her his arm.*

Up you go.

EUGENIA (*icily*): Thank you, Judas!

EUGENE: Your cards were no good anyway.

EUGENIA: Fool!

ARTHUR: This ought to cure you of your disgusting frivolity. (*Tapping his pockets.*) Matches! Who's got a match?

EUGENIA (*lying down on the catafalque*): At least spare me the candles, Arthur.

ARTHUR: Quiet, or I'll think up something really grim.

EDDIE (*without taking his eyes off the book, produces a box of matches*): Here!

ARTHUR *takes the matches, lights the candles.* EUGENE *takes the artificial flowers from the table, places them beside* EUGENIA, *takes a few steps back to examine the effect, adjusts the flowers again.*

Great pictures! (*He giggles.*)

EUGENIA (*raising her head*): What's he looking at?

ARTHUR: Lie down!

EUGENE (*steps up to* EDDIE *and looks over his shoulder*): *Handbook of Anatomy.*

EUGENIA: Just what he needs!

EDDIE: Is Mr. Arthur studying medicine?

EUGENE: He's studying for three different degrees. One in philosophy.

EDDIE: Is there something like this for philosophy?

EUGENE: Don't be ridiculous! They don't illustrate philosophy.

EDDIE: Too bad. It might be good.

EUGENIA (*sitting up*): Let me see!

ARTHUR: Lie down!

EUGENIA: To think that you're the youngest one of us all! Why don't you enter a monastery?

ARTHUR: Why do you simply refuse to understand me, Grandmother?

EUGENE: Yes, I've been wondering about that myself. Why do you refuse to understand him, Eugenia?

ARTHUR: I just can't live in a world like this!

ELEANOR *enters from the door on the extreme left. She has definitely crossed the threshold of middle age. She is wearing slacks with suspenders in the style of the 1930's.*

ELEANOR: What kind of world? What *are* you people doing?

ARTHUR: Good morning, Mother.

ELEANOR: Mama! On the catafalque again?

EUGENIA: A good thing you've come, Eleanor. Now you can see for yourself how he treats me.

ARTHUR: How *I* treat *you?* She had to be disciplined.

EUGENIA: He's trying to educate me.

ARTHUR: She really goes too far.

ELEANOR: What did she do?

ARTHUR: She knows.

ELEANOR: But why the catafalque?

ARTHUR: To remind her of eternity. Let her lie there and look within.

ELEANOR (*seeing* EDDIE): Ah, Eddie.

EDDIE: Hi!

ARTHUR: You mean you know each other?

EUGENE (*to himself*): Here we go.

ELEANOR: Everybody knows Eddie. Why not?

ARTHUR: I'm going mad. I come home and what do I find? Laxity, chaos, shady characters, ambiguous relationships. And on top of all that, it turns out that even you . . . No! No! Why does all this have to happen? Where is it all going to end?

ELEANOR: Perhaps you'd like something to eat?

ARTHUR: Eat? No. All I want is to get the situation under control.

ELEANOR: Oh Lord. I sleep with Eddie from time to time. Don't I, Eddie?

EDDIE (*absently*): What? Oh yes. Of course. (*He unfolds some color plates inserted in the book.*) Look at that! And all in color!

ARTHUR: What's that? What did you say, Mother?

ELEANOR: I'll get you something to eat. I won't be long.

She goes out through the door right rear. ARTHUR *sits down distraught.*

EUGENE (*to himself*): She did put that a bit bluntly. I must say. (*To* ARTHUR.) May I take this off now? (*Silence.*) Arthur? (*Silence.*) Arthur! (*Silence.*) Arthur, I say, may I take this thing off now?

ARTHUR: Take it off. (*To himself.*) Nothing matters now.

EUGENE (*taking the bird cage off his head*): Thank you! (*He sits down next to* ARTHUR.) What's wrong, Arthur?

EUGENIA: Christ, this thing is hard!

EUGENE: I can understand that this business about your mother must be rather upsetting. I can well understand that. I'm an old-timer. (*Pause.*) Eddie's not a bad sort. He has a good heart even if he doesn't look very bright. (*More softly.*) Between you and me, he's not quite all there. . . . (*Louder.*) But what can you expect, my dear boy? Life must be taken as it is . . . (*more softly*) . . . or must it? (*Louder.*) Now, now, Arthur. Chin up! Eddie has his good points, and after all, my goodness . . . we've got to face up to it: your mother isn't quite what she used to be. (*More softly.*) You should have seen her when she was young, before you were born, of course. Even before Stomil came along . . . (*Ponders, moves his chair closer to* ARTHUR; *very softly.*) What are you planning to do about Eddie anyway? Frankly, he's a thoroughly bad sort. His fingernails are always so dirty. A sleazy type, wouldn't you say? And I'm convinced that he cheats at cards. He smacks his lips when he eats and he goes around here as if he owned the place. I wouldn't even shake hands with him if I weren't afraid of offending Eugenia. You know what he did yesterday? I go to Eugenia and I say: "Look here, it's fine with me if Eddie doesn't brush his teeth, but if he has to borrow my tooth-brush, I wish he'd brush his teeth with it instead of his shoes." And what does he say? "There's nothing wrong with my teeth. They're white. They're sharp. But sometimes my shoes get dirty." That's what he says and then throws me out. I wouldn't want to influence you one way or another, but if I were you, I'd get rid of him. How about throwing him down the stairs? Hm?

ARTHUR: Oh, that wouldn't really solve anything.

EUGENE: Or maybe a left hook right in the face?

ARTHUR: That, too, would leave the basic situation un-changed.

EUGENE: Just a small one right in the face? It couldn't do any harm. If it's all right with you, I'll tell him to get ready for one.

EUGENIA *has meanwhile sat up and is listening. As soon as* EUGENE *notices this, he moves away from* ARTHUR. *Louder.*

Eddie is simple, yes, simple and very decent. I have never in all my years met a simpler man.

EUGENIA: What's wrong with him?

EUGENE: I don't know. He just doesn't react anymore.

EUGENIA: What are you whispering in his ear?

EUGENE: Me? Nothing. I've just been telling him about the life of the bees.

ELEANOR (*brings in a tray with a cup and cookies*): Break-fast is ready, Arthur!

ARTHUR (*waking out of his thoughts; automatically*): Thank you, Mother.

He sits down at the table. ELEANOR *sets the tray down in front of him, roughly shoving other objects aside.* ARTHUR *stirs his coffee. The tray is tilted up. He pulls a woman's shoe out from under it and heaves it angrily into the corner.*

EDDIE: Could you let me have this until Tuesday?

ARTHUR: I'm afraid not. I've got an exam on Monday.

EDDIE: Too bad. Some terrific pictures in here.

ELEANOR: Mother, get down off that thing, will you? You look like a character out of Edgar Allen Poe.

EUGENIA: A who, out of what?

ELEANOR: Oh, just like somebody on a catafalque. It's all so terribly old-fashioned.

EUGENIA (*motioning toward* ARTHUR): But what will he say?

ELEANOR: He's eating now. He won't say anything.

EUGENIA: Arthur, may I get down?

ARTHUR: It's all the same to me. (*He drinks.*) This coffee's bitter.

ELEANOR: We're all out of sugar. Eugene ate it.

EUGENE: I beg your pardon. All I ate was the jam. It was Eddie who ate up the sugar.

EUGENIA *comes down from the catafalque.*

ELEANOR: And blow those candles out, will you? We've got to economize. (*Looking at the cards.*) Who's winning?

EUGENIA: Eddie.

EUGENE: There is something positively unnatural about Edward's good luck.

ELEANOR: Eddie, have you been cheating?

EDDIE: Me? Never.

ELEANOR: You haven't? But you promised you'd lose today, remember? I need the money for groceries.

EDDIE (*throwing up his arms*): I must be a born winner. Tough luck!

Enter STOMIL, *Arthur's father. In pajamas, sleepy. Yawning and scratching himself. He is a large, corpulent man with gray hair like a lion's mane.*

STOMIL: I smelled coffee. (*Catching sight of* EDDIE.) Hello, Eddie.

ARTHUR *thrusts the tray aside and observes the scene with tense interest.*

ELEANOR: I thought this was your day to sleep until noon. The bed will be occupied after lunch.

STOMIL: I can't sleep. A whole new idea suddenly came to me. Who's drinking coffee anyway? Oh, it's you, Arthur . . . (*He steps up to the table.*)

ARTHUR (*disgustedly*): Good God, Father, can't you at least button up your pajamas?

STOMIL: What for?

ARTHUR: What for? What do you mean, what for?

STOMIL: I mean: What for? Such a simple question and you can't find an answer.

ARTHUR: Because . . . because one just doesn't appear like that.

STOMIL (*drinking Arthur's coffee*): You see? Your answer is meaningless. It's pure convention. It won't stand up under the scrutiny of the intellect.

ARTHUR: Isn't that enough?

STOMIL: Not at all. Not for me. I'm the kind of man who goes deeper. If we're going to discuss this, we've got to take the imponderables into account.

ARTHUR: Oh Lord, Father, can't you button your fly first and then talk it over?

STOMIL: That would be a complete reversal of the logical thought process. The effect would precede the cause. Man should never act without thinking, never act like an automaton.

ARTHUR: I take it then that you will not button your pajamas.

STOMIL: No, son. Anyway, I can't. No buttons.

He takes a swallow of coffee. He sets the cup down on the table. Unnoticed, EDDIE *has crept up behind* ARTHUR.

ARTHUR: I might have expected as much.

STOMIL: Not at all. In this case at least, matter springs from the mind.

EDDIE *reaches over Arthur's shoulder for the cup and drinks.*

ARTHUR: That's precisely what I wanted to talk to you about, Father.

STOMIL: Later, boy. Later. (*Takes a swallow out of the cup which is now in front of* EDDIE. *Looks toward the cata- falque.*) Isn't anybody ever going to remove that thing?

ELEANOR: Why?

STOMIL: Well, I have nothing against it on purely formal grounds. Actually it enriches reality, stimulates the imagination. But I could use the space for my ex- periments.

ELEANOR: But you've got the whole house.

EUGENIA: I'd be glad, too, if you got rid of it. Then Arthur couldn't torture me.

ARTHUR (*pounding the table with his fist*): You see? What's going on in this house? Chaos, anarchy, entropy! How long has it been since Grandfather died? Ten years!

And all that time nobody's ever thought of ridding the house of that catafalque. Incredible! We should be grateful, though, that you at least took Grandfather out of the house.

EUGENE: We couldn't keep Grandfather any longer.

ARTHUR: I'm not interested in the details. It's the principle of the thing.

STOMIL (*drinking coffee, bored*): Really?

ARTHUR (*jumps up and runs across the stage*): But it's not only Grandfather. I was born twenty-five years ago and my baby carriage is still standing here. (*He kicks the baby carriage.*) Why isn't it up in the attic? And what's this thing? Mother's wedding dress. (*He pulls the dusty veil from under a pile of rubbish.*) Why isn't it put away in a closet? And Uncle Eugene's riding breeches. What are they lying around here for when the last horse he ever rode died forty years ago? No order, no sense of reality, no decency, no initiative. You can't move in this place, you can't breathe, you can't live!

Taking advantage of the confusion, EDDIE *empties the cup at one gulp.*

ELEANOR (*aside to* EDDIE): How beautifully you drink, Eddie!

STOMIL: My boy, tradition doesn't interest me in the slightest. Your indignation is absurd. You know very well we attach no importance to these monuments of the past, these relics of family tradition. That's why everything's lying around like this. We live in freedom. (*He looks into the cup.*) Where's my coffee?

ARTHUR: No, no, Father, you just don't understand me. That's not what bothers me. No, that's not it.

STOMIL: Then kindly explain yourself more clearly, will you, boy? (*To* ELEANOR.) Isn't there any more coffee?

ELEANOR: No, there won't be any until the day after to-morrow.

STOMIL: Why the day after tomorrow?

ELEANOR: How should I know?

STOMIL: All right. Never mind.

ARTHUR: Listen to me! It's not this particular tradition that bothers me. It's a fact that in this family there's no frame of reference at all. All that's left is bits and pieces, fragments, rubbish. You've destroyed everything but you go on destroying; you've gone on so long you've finally forgotten why you began in the first place.

ELEANOR: He's right. Stomil, do you still remember how we shattered tradition? How, in protest against tradition, I gave myself to you with Mummy and Daddy looking on? In the first row of the orchestra at the opening night of *Tannhäuser*. What a gorgeous scandal that was! Where are the days when people were still shocked by such things? And then you proposed to me.

STOMIL: As I recall it was at the National Museum's first avant-garde exhibition. The critics gave us rave reviews.

ELEANOR: No. It was at the opera. At the exhibition it wasn't you, or maybe it wasn't me. You're getting everything mixed up.

STOMIL: Possibly. (*With enthusiasm.*) The days of revolt, the time of the great leap forward. Liberation from the fetters of the old art and the old way of life. Man coming into his own, man overthrowing the old gods and putting himself on the pedestal. The seed burst open, the chains snapped. Revolution and release. That was our slogan then. Away with outmoded forms,

down with convention! Long live the dynamic! Life
as creation, an incessant striving toward new frontiers!
Movement and struggle! All form transcended!

ELEANOR: Stomil! You've been drinking at the fountain of
youth! I hardly recognize you.

STOMIL: Yes, we were young once.

ELEANOR: What do you mean? We haven't grown any
older. We've never betrayed our ideals. Why, even
now our motto is still: Forward! Ever forward!

STOMIL (*without enthusiasm*): Yes. Yes. That's right.

ELEANOR: Do we have any prejudices? Do conventions mean
anything to us? Aren't we still fighting against the old?
Aren't we free?

STOMIL: The old what?

ELEANOR: Well, the old times. Don't you remember? Don't
tell me you've forgotten what we were just talking
about? All those fetters, those rusty chains of religion,
morality, society, art. Especially art, Stomil. Art!

STOMIL: Yes, of course. But when was all that actually?

ELEANOR: Just a minute. Let me figure it out. We were
married in 1900 . . . no, just let me think . . . Arthur was
born in 1930, or . . . oh, be quiet, will you? Or was it
1940?

STOMIL: Oh, *then*. I see. (*He stops in front of the mirror,
passes his hand over his face.*)

ELEANOR: Don't interrupt me. You're getting me all mixed
up . . . (*Figures in an undertone, thoroughly ab-
sorbed.*) 1914 . . . 1918 . . . 1921 . . .

STOMIL (*at the mirror*): We're young. Eternally young . . .

ARTHUR: Father's right.

STOMIL: What do you mean?

ARTHUR: It's all dead and gone now. All in the past.

ELEANOR *runs across the stage, whispering dates, becoming more and more entangled in her calculations.*

STOMIL: What's gone?

ARTHUR: All those fetters and chains! They're all gone now, unfortunately.

STOMIL: Unfortunately? You don't know what you're saying. If you'd lived in those days, you'd know how much we've done for you. You have no idea what the world was like then. Can you imagine how much courage it took to dance the tango? Do you realize that in those days there were hardly any fallen women? That the only recognized style of painting was naturalism? That the theater was utterly bourgeois? Stifling. Insufferable. You couldn't even put your elbows down on the dinner table! I can still remember a youth demonstration on that very issue. Why, it wasn't until after 1900 that the boldest, the most advanced spirits stopped giving up their seats to elderly people. No, we didn't spare ourselves in our struggle for these rights and if you today can push your grandmother around, its to us your thanks are due. You simply can't imagine how much you owe us. To think how we struggled to give you this freedom which you now despise!

ARTHUR: And what did you do with it? What did you produce? This bawdyhouse where nothing works because everyone can do what he pleases, where there are no laws and no violations?

STOMIL: I know only one law: Don't hesitate, do what you feel like. Every man is entitled to his own kind of happiness.

ELEANOR: Stomil, I've got it! I've figured it out! It was 1928.

STOMIL: What was?

ELEANOR (*in consternation*): I've forgotten.

ARTHUR: You've poisoned the generations before you and after you with your freedom. Look at Grandmother! She's completely addled. Haven't you noticed?

EUGENIA: I just knew he'd drag me into it.

STOMIL: There's nothing wrong with Mama. What do you mean?

ARTHUR: Naturally you're not shocked by her senile demoralization. Once she was a dignified, self-respecting grandmother. And now? Now she plays poker with Eddie!

EDDIE: I beg your pardon. We also play bridge, you know.

ARTHUR: I wasn't talking to you.

STOMIL: Each has the right to do what he wants and with whomever he chooses. Old people too.

ARTHUR: That's not a right. It's a moral obligation to be immoral.

STOMIL: You astonish me. Your opinions are so terribly outdated. When we were your age, we considered every kind of conformity disgraceful. Rebellion! Rebellion alone had any value for us.

ARTHUR: What value?

STOMIL: A dynamic and therefore positive value, though sometimes in a negative way. I trust you don't think we were merely blind anarchists? Certainly not. We were a column marching off to the future, a movement, a historical process. History is indebted to us. What is rebellion? The rock on which progress builds its temple and the greater the scope of the rebellion the grander the temple will be. Believe me: the scope of our rebellion was prodigious.

ARTHUR: But if that's the case . . . why these misunderstand-

ings? If you too are trying to do something construc-
tive, why can't we build together?

STOMIL: Impossible. What I said just now was purely objective. I described our historical role, but said nothing
of our intentions. Well then, what were our intentions? Why, to do what we wanted, go our own ways,
each for himself. We have always pursued our own in-
clinations. But by opposing everything, we paved the
way for the future.

ARTHUR: What future?

STOMIL: That's not my affair. My job was to shatter exist-
ing forms.

ARTHUR: In other words, we're still enemies?

STOMIL: Why take it so tragically? All you need to do
is stop worrying about principles.

ELEANOR: Yes. What I still can't understand is why you,
the youngest of us all, should be the one to harp on
principles. It used to be the other way around.

ARTHUR: Because I'm starting out in the world. But what a
world! If I want a world, I've got to make one.

STOMIL: But you're young, Arthur. Don't you want to be
modern? At your age?

ARTHUR: That's just the point. These modern times of
yours. Even Grandmother has grown old in this world
that has lost its standards. That's how modern your era
is. What's more, you've grown old in it.

EUGENE: If you'll allow me to put in a word, I should like
to call your attention to certain achievements, for instance, the right to wear short pants . . . ah, the fresh
feel of the breeze . . .

ARTHUR: Oh, keep quiet, Uncle. Don't you realize that,
precisely because everything is possible, nothing is
possible anymore? If you were at least bucking conven-

tion with your short pants. But all convention was broken ages ago. By the time you came along it was all taken care of. The whole thing is absurd.

STOMIL: Well, what *do* you want then? Tradition?

ARTHUR: An orderly world!

STOMIL: That's all?

ARTHUR: . . . and the right to rebel.

STOMIL: That's it. That's what I've been telling you all along: *rebel!*

ARTHUR: Don't you see that you've deprived me of every last chance to revolt? You've been nonconformists so long that there aren't any conventions left to rebel against. You've left nothing for me . . . nothing! Your only norm is the absence of all norms. The only thing left for me to rebel against is you . . . you and your immorality.

STOMIL: Go right ahead. Did I ever tell you not to?

EUGENE: That's the stuff, Arthur. You'll show them.

ELEANOR: Maybe it would calm you down. You've been so jittery lately. . . .

EUGENIA *makes signs to* EDDIE; *they come to an understanding behind Arthur's back and pick up the cards.*

ARTHUR (*falls into an armchair with resignation*): Impossible!

ELEANOR: Why?

EUGENE: We're all in favor of it.

ARTHUR: Rebel against you? What are you anyway? A formless mass, an amorphous blob, an atomized world, a mob without shape or structure. Your world can't even be blown up; it's disintegrated all by itself.

STOMIL: You mean we're no good for anything?

ARTHUR: Exactly.

ELEANOR: But couldn't you just try?

ARTHUR: There's nothing to try. It's hopeless. You're all so disgustingly tolerant.

STOMIL: Yes, that could be irritating, I suppose. Still, I don't like to see you feeling so left out.

ELEANOR (*stands behind him and strokes his hair*): Poor little Arthur. You mustn't think your mother's heart is made of stone.

EUGENE: We all love you, Arthur. We want to help you.

EUGENIA (*to* EDDIE): I pass.

ARTHUR: It's hopeless. This nonconformism you're pushing me into is only a new kind of conformism. But I can't be a conformist forever. I'm twenty-five. My friends are all laughing at me.

STOMIL: But what about art, Arthur? What about art?

ELEANOR: Exactly. You've taken the words out of my mouth.

ARTHUR: What art?

STOMIL: Well, art in general. I've devoted my whole life to art. Art is eternal rebellion. Why don't you give it a try?

EDDIE: Bring your bedding. Skip the wedding.

EUGENIA: Crash, smash, I'm out of cash.

ARTHUR: Father, you bore me. I want to be a doctor.

ELEANOR: A disgrace to the whole family! I've always dreamed of his becoming an artist. When I was carrying him in my womb, I ran through the woods stark naked, singing Bach. All for nothing!

ARTHUR: Maybe you sang out of tune.

STOMIL: All the same, don't give up hope. You still don't understand the value of art. I've just had an idea for a new experiment. You'll see.

ELEANOR (*clapping her hands*): Eugenia, Eddie. Stomil has come up with something new.

EUGENIA: Again?

STOMIL: Yes. It came to me this morning. It's absolutely original.

ELEANOR: You'll put it on right away, won't you, Stomil?

STOMIL: I'm ready.

EUGENE: Heaven help us!

ELEANOR: Eugene, move the table. Make room.

EUGENE *shoves the table aside with a good deal of crashing and thumping.* EUGENIA *and* EDDIE *pick up the cards and step to one side. Under the mound of draperies suggesting a bed, something starts to move. Finally Cousin Ala's head comes to light.*

ALA (*a girl of eighteen with a good figure and long hair. She blinks in the light and yawns*): Where am I? First all that shouting and now they're moving furniture . . . What time is it anyway?

ARTHUR: Ala!

ELEANOR: I forgot to tell you, Ala has been here since six o'clock this morning.

STOMIL: This is marvelous, Ala. You're just in time for the show. (*To* EUGENE.) That's fine. Now the catafalque.

ARTHUR: But why didn't you tell me? If I'd known, I'd have kept them quiet.

He notices that EDDIE *is approaching* ALA *with interest.*

Back Eddie. Face to the wall.

EDDIE *steps back obediently and stands with his face to the wall.*

Did you sleep well?

ALA: So so.

ARTHUR: How long can you stay?

ALA: I don't know. I told Mother I might never go back.

ARTHUR: And what did she say?

ALA: Nothing. She wasn't there.

ARTHUR: Then how could you tell her?

ALA: Maybe I didn't. I don't remember.

ARTHUR: You've forgotten?

ALA: It was so long ago.

ARTHUR: How about some breakfast? Oh! We're out of coffee. May I sit beside you?

ALA: Why not?

> ARTHUR *gets a chair and sits down beside the pile of draperies.*

ARTHUR: You're very lovely.

> ALA *laughs loudly.*

What are you laughing about?

ALA (*suddenly stops laughing. Gloomily*): Me? Laughing? I'm not laughing.

ARTHUR: But you *were.*

ALA: Are you trying to pick a fight?

ARTHUR: I've been thinking about you a lot, Ala.

ALA (*loud and coarse*): Go on.

ARTHUR: I thought about meeting you!

ALA: Go on.

ARTHUR: And sitting down beside you . . .

ALA: Go on.

ARTHUR: . . . and talking with you . . .

ALA (*gradually growing excited as though watching a boxing match*): Go on.

ARTHUR: . . . about one thing and another . . .

ALA: Go on.
ARTHUR (*louder*): About different kinds of things.
ALA: Go on! Go on!

ARTHUR *picks up the book that* EDDIE *has left on the chair and throws it at* ALA. *She dodges and hides under the covers.*

ARTHUR: Come out!
ALA (*sticking her head out*): What's wrong with you?

ARTHUR *says nothing.*

Why did you do that?

ARTHUR *says nothing.*

What do you want anyway?
ARTHUR: That's what they all keep asking me.
ALA: Never mind. I don't need to know.
STOMIL: Kindly take your seats. Kindly take your seats.

The stage is set for Stomil's experiment. To one side, the table. Nearer the proscenium, four chairs are lined up with their backs to the audience. EUGENIA, ELEANOR *and* EUGENE *sit down from left to right.* EDDIE *picks up his bottle of beer, still half-full, and tries to tiptoe away.* EUGENE *sees him and points him out to* ELEANOR.

ELEANOR: Eddie, where are you going?
EDDIE: Be back in a minute.
ELEANOR: You stay right here!

EDDIE *turns around with resignation, sits down on the chair to the right of* EUGENE, *intentionally stepping on his foot.* STOMIL *goes into the room opening into the corridor on the left-hand side of the stage.*

Arthur, Ala, what are you doing? We're waiting for you.

ALA: What's going on?

ARTHUR: Experimental drama. You know my father.

He gives her his hand. ALA *jumps up. She has on a long nightgown that reaches the floor. It should not be transparent—this is called expressly to the attention of directors who like to make things easy for themselves. The cut and ruching make it look almost like a dress. They stand beside the chair on the extreme right.* EDDIE *stretches out his arm and takes* ALA *by the waist.* ARTHUR *changes places with her.*

STOMIL (*who has meanwhile come back with a big box and gone behind the catafalque so that only his head can be seen*): Ladies and gentlemen, your attention please. Here are the principal characters of our drama. (*In the tone of a circus director introducing the next number.*) Adam and Eve in paradise! (*Over the catafalque which serves as the stage, two puppets manipulated by* STOMIL *are seen: Adam and Eve, with the apple in her hand.*)

EUGENE: We've had that.

STOMIL (*in consternation*): When?

EUGENE: At the beginning of the world.

STOMIL: That was the old version. This is a new one.

EDDIE: Where's the snake?

ELEANOR (*whispering*): Shhh!

STOMIL: The snake is in our imagination. We all know the story. Attention please! Here we go! (*In a deep voice.*)

So this is Paradise.
I'm Adam and before me lies

A world of possibilities.
But now it starts. From Adam's bone
Eve steps upon the earth.
To what will *she* give birth?
O Destiny, 'tis known
To you alone.

(*In a soprano.*)

Adam was first, but he
Did not exist until
I also came to be.
He walks so proudly still.
Doesn't the poor man see
For all his intellection
That there is no perfection
Except in what is not?
Where does the darkness go
When the sun comes out?
O Destiny!

A *loud report and all the lights go out.*

ELEANOR'S VOICE: Stomil, Stomil, what's happened? You're not dead, are you?
EUGENE'S VOICE: Fire! Fire!

ARTHUR *lights a match and then the candles over the catafalque.* STOMIL *appears, he is holding an enormous revolver.*

STOMIL: Well, what do you say? Not bad, eh?
ELEANOR: Stomil, you frightened us so!
STOMIL: Every experiment must shock. That's my first principle.
EUGENE: If that's what you were after, it was a success all right. My heart's still pounding.

ELEANOR: How did you do it, Stomil?

STOMIL: I unscrewed the fuse and fired the revolver.

ELEANOR: Marvelous!

EUGENE: What's so marvelous about it?

STOMIL: Don't you understand?

EUGENE: No, I don't.

ELEANOR: Don't mind him, Stomil. Eugene has always been slow.

STOMIL: How about you, Eugenia?

EUGENIA: Huh?

STOMIL (*louder*): Did you understand the experiment, Mama?

ELEANOR: The experiment has made her deaf.

EUGENE: That doesn't surprise me.

STOMIL: Let me explain. The shock method creates an immediate unity of action and perception. See?

EUGENE: Yes, but . . .

STOMIL: Yes, but what?

EUGENE: But what's that got to do with Adam and Eve?

ELEANOR: Eugene, do try to concentrate.

STOMIL: What we are dealing with here is an intrinsically theatrical phenomenon, the dynamics of sense perception. That means something to you, doesn't it?

EUGENE: Frankly, I don't think it does.

STOMIL (*throws the revolver on the catafalque*): I give up.

ELEANOR: Don't be discouraged, Stomil. Who's going to experiment if you lose heart?

All stand up and put the chairs back in their places.

EUGENE: A flop, friends.

EDDIE: Give me the movies.

ELEANOR: Well, now what should we do?

ARTHUR: Clear out! All of you. Out!

STOMIL: What's got into you?

ARTHUR: All of you! I can't bear the sight of you.

STOMIL: Is that a way to treat your own father?

ARTHUR: I used to have a father. Not anymore. I'll have to make myself a father.

STOMIL: You? *You* make *me?*

ARTHUR: You and the whole lot of you. I'm going to make you all over. And now get out. This minute!

STOMIL: That boy's going just a bit too far.

ELEANOR: Never mind, Stomil. Thank God, we're enlightened.

STOMIL: You think I should really go?

ELEANOR: Why not? After all, you're not really interested in anything but your experiments.

STOMIL: Ah yes, art! Modern art! Give me God and I'll make an experiment out of Him.

ELEANOR: There. You see!

They all go out through the door left rear.

EDDIE (*to* EUGENIA): Come on, Grandma.

EUGENIA: Don't forget the cards.

EDDIE picks up the cards and goes out with EUGENIA.

EDDIE (*turning around again, to* ARTHUR): If you need anything . . .

ARTHUR (*stamping his foot*): Get out!

EDDIE (*conciliatory*): Okay, okay!

He goes out left with EUGENIA.

EUGENE (*after making sure that the others are gone*): You're absolutely right, Arthur. Between you and me, they're a bad lot.

ARTHUR: You too. Out!

EUGENE: Certainly. Certainly, my boy. I'm going. I only wanted to tell you that you can count on me.

ARTHUR: What do you mean?

EUGENE: Never mind. Just do what you think right. But remember. I can be useful to you. I'm not as far gone as the rest of them. (*More softly.*) I'm an old-timer.

ARTHUR: Glad to hear it. But now leave us alone, will you?

EUGENE (*goes out left, turns around again and says with emphasis*): An old-timer. (*Exits.*)

ALA: Now what?

ARTHUR: Now I'll explain everything.

Stefan Schnabel as Stomil

Elizabeth Swain as Ala

Lilyan Wilbur as Eleanor, David Margulies as Arthur, Stefan Schnabel as Stomil, Elizabeth Swain as Ala

ACT TWO

The same scene as in Act One. The only light comes from a simple standing lamp. ARTHUR *is sitting in an armchair. Someone enters from the right.*

ARTHUR: Who's there?
FIGURE: Me.
ARTHUR: Who's me?
FIGURE: Your Uncle Eugene.
ARTHUR: Password?
EUGENE: New life. Countersign?
ARTHUR: Rebirth. (*Pause.*) All right. Come in.

> EUGENE *steps into the light. He sits down facing* ARTHUR.

EUGENE: Oof. I'm exhausted.
ARTHUR: Is everything ready?
EUGENE: I've brought everything I could down from the attic. You should see the moths! You think it will work?
ARTHUR: It's got to work.
EUGENE: I'm worried, worried. They're so demoralized . . . Think of it. A whole lifetime in this bawdy-house . . . I beg your pardon, I meant this atmosphere of moral disintegration. You see, it's contagious. Forgive me.
ARTHUR: Forget it. What's my father doing?
EUGENE: He's in his room, working on a new production. Don't you feel sorry for him sometimes? After all, he actually believes in that art of his.

ARTHUR: Then why do you discourage him?

EUGENE: For spite. To get his goat. But the fact is, those experiments of his don't mean a thing to me. What do you make of them?

ARTHUR: I've got other problems. And Mother?

EUGENE *stands up, goes to the door left rear and looks through the keyhole.*

EUGENE: Can't see a thing. Either she's turned the light out or hung something over the keyhole. (*He goes back to his former place.*)

ARTHUR: And Grandmother Eugenia?

EUGENE: Probably sitting at her mirror, putting on makeup.

ARTHUR: Good. You may go now. I have an important appointment in a few minutes.

EUGENE (*stands up*): Any further orders?

ARTHUR: Be vigilant. Eyes open, mouth shut, and ready for action.

EUGENE: Yes, sir. (*On his way out.*) God protect you, Arthur, my boy . . . Maybe we'll manage to bring the good old days back again yet.

Goes out to the right. ALA *enters by way of the corridor right. She is still wearing her nightgown.*

ALA (*yawning*): What did you want me for?

ARTHUR: Shh . . . quiet.

ALA: Why?

ARTHUR: This is private—between you and me.

ALA: You think they care what we do? We could climb up the walls and sleep on the ceiling for all they care. (*She sits down, wincing as though in pain.*)

ARTHUR: What's wrong?

ALA: Stomil pinched me twice today.

ARTHUR: The rotter!

ALA: Arthur, he's your father!

ARTHUR (*kissing her hand gallantly*): Thank you for reminding me.

ALA: It sounds so old-fashioned, nobody calls his father a rotter nowadays.

ARTHUR: What *do* you call him then?

ALA: Nothing. You just ignore him.

ARTHUR (*disappointed*): Then I was mistaken.

ALA: Well, it's your headache that he's your father. Personally, I think he's great.

ARTHUR (*contemptuously*): An artist!

ALA: What's wrong with that?

ARTHUR: Artists are a plague. They were the first to contaminate our society.

ALA (*bored*): Oh, who cares? (*Yawns.*) What did you want me for? It's cold in here. I'm practically naked. Hadn't you noticed?

ARTHUR: Well, what do you say? Have you thought it over?

ALA: You mean will I marry you? But I've already told you. I don't see the point.

ARTHUR: You mean the answer is no?

ALA: Why do you get so worked up about it? I mean—I don't care—if it means so much to you, we can get married tomorrow. We're already cousins.

ARTHUR: But I *want* you to care! I want you to realize that marriage is something very important.

ALA: Important? Why? I don't get it. If I'm going to have a baby it'll be with you, not with the minister. So what's the problem?

ARTHUR: Well, if it's not important in itself, then we've got to make it important.

ALA: What for?

ARTHUR: Nothing is important in itself. Things in themselves are meaningless. Unless we give them character, we drown in a sea of indifference. We have to create meanings, because they don't exist in nature.

ALA: But what for? What for?

ARTHUR: Well if you must have a reason, let's say: for our own pleasure and profit.

ALA: Pleasure?

ARTHUR: Yes. We derive pleasure from profit and we only profit from doing things we attach importance to—difficult things, the unusual things that seem rare and precious. And that's why we have to create a system of values.

ALA: Philosophy bores me. I think I prefer Stomil. (*She sticks her leg out from under the nightgown.*)

ARTHUR: You only think that. Kindly remove that leg.

ALA: You don't like it?

ARTHUR: That has nothing whatsoever to do with the subject.

ALA (*obstinately*): You really don't like it?

ARTHUR (*with difficulty takes his eyes off her leg*): Oh, all right, show your leg if you want to. Anyway, it only proves my point.

ALA: My leg? (*She examines her leg closely.*)

ARTHUR: Yes. Do you know why you're showing your leg? Because I don't leap all over you like my artist father and everybody else does. That worries you. You were pretty bewildered this morning when we were all alone. You thought you knew what I wanted from you.

ALA: That's not true.

ARTHUR: Not true? Ha. You think I didn't see how upset you were when I proposed marriage instead of just picking you up and throwing you down on the bed?

ALA: I had a headache.

ARTHUR: Headache? Go on. You just couldn't figure out *what* was going on. You thought I wasn't attracted, that you must be losing your charms. If I suddenly started acting like my father, it would be a relief, wouldn't it? Yes. Except you'd run away, just to get even with me.

ALA (*stands up with dignity*): I'm running all right.

ARTHUR (*takes her by the hand and pulls her down into the chair*): Sit down. I haven't finished yet. All you care about is your sex appeal. You're so primitive! You can't think about anything else. You don't know anything else!

ALA: Are you suggesting that I'm backward? (*She tries again to stand up.*)

ARTHUR (*holding her down*): You stay right here. You've confirmed my theory. My behavior was atypical; that baffled you. The unusual is a value in itself. See? I have given meaning to an encounter that would otherwise have meant nothing. I!

ALA: Well, if you're so terribly clever, what do you need me for? If you're so awfully superior, why don't you just live all by yourself?

ARTHUR: You don't have to be so touchy.

ALA: We'll see how far you get alone. Or with Uncle Eugene. (*She resolutely draws her nightgown over her knees, buttons it up to the neck, and wraps herself in a steamer rug. She puts on the bowler and draws it down deep over her forehead.*)

ARTHUR (*shyly*): Don't be angry.

ALA: What do you care?

Pause.

ARTHUR: Aren't you too warm . . . in that blanket?

ALA: No.

ARTHUR: Uncle Eugene's hat doesn't look very good on you.

ALA: I don't care.

ARTHUR: Suit yourself. Where were we anyway? Oh yes, a system of values . . . (*He moves his chair closer to* ALA.) Now, generally speaking, a system of values is indispensable to the proper functioning both of the individual and of society. (*He seizes Ala's hand.*) Without the right kind of values we can never hope to create a harmonious world or establish the necessary balance between those elements commonly termed good and evil—though of course I use these words in their larger rather than strictly ethical sense. Now in this connection our task is two-fold: We must, one, restore the practical relevance of these concepts and, two, formulate rules of conduct which . . .

He flings himself at ALA *and tries to kiss her. She struggles free; they wrestle.* EDDIE *enters with his towel around his neck and a hairnet on his head.*

EDDIE (*with the pretentious enunciation typical of the semi-literate*): Oh, do excuse me.

ARTHUR (*lets* ALA *go as if nothing had happened.* ALA *straightens her hat and rubs her shoulder demonstratively*): What are *you* doing here?

EDDIE: I was just going to the kitchen for a drink of water. I beg your pardon, I didn't know you were conversing.

ARTHUR: Water? Water? What for?

EDDIE (*with dignity*): Because I'm thirsty, sir.

ARTHUR: At this hour? In the middle of the night?

EDDIE (*offended*): If that's the way you feel about it, I can go without.

ARTHUR (*furious*): Drink and get out!

EDDIE: As you wish. (*He goes majestically to the door left rear.*)

ARTHUR: Just a minute.

EDDIE: Yes, sir?

ARTHUR: The kitchen is on the right.

EDDIE: There? Impossible.

ARTHUR: I believe I know where the kitchen is in my own house.

EDDIE: You just can't be sure of anything these days. (*He changes his direction and goes out through the door right rear.*)

ARTHUR: That idiot! I'll have to take care of him once and for all.

ALA (*icily*): Have you finished taking care of me?

ARTHUR: It's all his fault.

ALA: I suppose it was his fault you nearly twisted my arm off.

ARTHUR: Does it hurt very much?

ALA: What do you care?

She affects a cry of pain. ARTHUR, *troubled, tries to examine her shoulder.*

ARTHUR: Where does it hurt? (*He touches her shoulder, but not with his original purpose.*)

ALA (*uncovering her shoulder*): Here . . .

ARTHUR: I'm terribly sorry.

ALA (*uncovering her back*): . . . and here . . .

ARTHUR (*dismayed*): Really, I didn't mean to . . .

ALA (*thrusts her leg forward*): . . . and here . . .

ARTHUR: How can I ever make it up to you? . . .

ALA (*lays her forefinger on her rib*): . . . and here too!

ARTHUR: Forgive me. I didn't mean to . . .

ALA: Now you've shown what you really are—a brute. First a lot of talk and then the usual. (*She sinks tragically into an armchair.*) We poor women! Is it our fault we have bodies? If we could only check them somewhere like a hat or a coat. Then maybe we'd be safe from our sweet-talking cousins. Frankly, I'm surprised. You with your noble ideals.

ARTHUR (*confused*): But really, I . . .

ALA: No excuses! You don't think I like a good conversation too? But that calls for a nice restful atmosphere. How can I converse when some philosopher is clutching at my legs? But never mind. What were we talking about? It was just beginning to be interesting when you . . .

Behind the door through which EDDIE *has passed a sound of gushing water is heard. Then gargling.*

ARTHUR: This is too much. Do you seriously think I wanted to rape you?

ALA (*alarmed*): Didn't you?

ARTHUR: Certainly not. I was only teaching you a lesson.

ALA: Thanks. I know that subject.

ARTHUR: You can only think about one thing. Then why did you resist? Come on. Why?

ALA: You're vulgar.

ARTHUR: Science knows no shame. Why?

ALA: Well, why did you attack me?

ARTHUR: Attack you? I was sacrificing myself.

ALA: What?

ARTHUR: Yes, sacrificing myself in my effort to make certain things clear to you. It was a pure exercise in sexual pragmatics.

ALA: Pig! Scientific pig! Pragmatics? What is it anyway?

Some new kind of perversion?

ARTHUR: There's nothing new about it. I'm sure we'll always be friends. Yes, women will follow me.

ALA: Women? Which women?

ARTHUR: All women. Women throughout the world will be my allies. And once the women are convinced, the men will soon come around.

ALA: What women? Anybody I know? Anyway, do what you like with them. I couldn't care less.

ARTHUR: Look here. The central fact of history is the total enslavement of women, children and artists by men.

ALA: I thought you didn't approve of artists.

ARTHUR: That's beside the point. The reason men don't like artists is that artists aren't men. That's what has always brought artists and women together—unfortunately. The ideas men have dreamed up—like honor, logic, progress—have always been foreign to women and artists. It's only very recently that the male has even begun to suspect the existence of such things as ambiguity, relativity, forgetfulness—in short, the glamor and poetry of this world, the exact opposite of what he had originally invented in that thick soldier's skull of his and tried to impose on women, children and artists.

ALA: But what about you? Aren't you a male?

ARTHUR: I transcend myself; I take an objective view. That's essential if I'm to carry out my plan.

ALA: Can I trust you?

ARTHUR: It was only to make up for their lack of imagination that men invented the concept of honor. And, at the same time, of effeminacy. Why? To guarantee male solidarity. Anyone who dared question the code of manly virtues was immediately accused of being effeminate. The result was that, in self-defense, women, children and artists closed ranks to form a single community. They had no choice. . . . Just a second.

The gargling is still heard from the kitchen. ARTHUR *goes to the kitchen door.*

ALA: Maybe he's washing.

ARTHUR: Him? Not likely! (*He goes back to his place.*) Let's get back to the subject.

ALA: I just don't believe you. I see what you're getting at. You can't fool me.

ARTHUR: I have no desire to fool you. I'm simply trying to make you aware of your own interests as a woman.

ALA: What does that mean? You want me to strip?

ARTHUR: Oh, don't be tedious. Once you've finally come to see that our interests coincide, you'll be willing to work with me. What do men want? They want to abolish all conventions relating to sex. And why? To make life easier for *them*, to do away with all barriers between desire and satisfaction.

ALA: You've got something there. They jump you like a bull. Like you did just now.

ARTHUR: I can't deny that as an individual I'm subject to natural drives. But I have a higher goal. Taking advantage of the general breakdown in values, men have done everything they could to do away with the last remaining rules governing sexual behavior. I can't believe that women really like it, and that's the basis of my plan.

ALA: I like it fine.

ARTHUR: That's a lie. You *can't.*

ALA: Yes, I like it. It means I'm free, I can do as I please. For instance, if I take my clothes off right now, what can you do about it? (*She throws off the steamer rug and removes her hat.*)

ARTHUR: Stop it. This is a serious discussion.

ALA (*undoing the ribbons of her nightgown*): Why should I? Who's going to stop me? You? My mother? God? (*She bares her shoulders.*)

ARTHUR: Cover yourself this minute! Pull up that nightgown. (*He tries desperately to look away.*)

ALA: I will not. It's my nightgown.

Eddie's head is seen in the doorway.

Oh, hi, Eddie. Come on in.

ARTHUR (*pushing* EDDIE *away*): Get out or I'll kill you. Taking your clothes off in front of this . . . Have you no shame?

ALA: He may not be very cultured, but he has marvelous eyes.

ARTHUR: Eyes like a pig.

ALA: *I* like them.

ARTHUR: I'll kill him.

ALA (*sweetly*): You wouldn't be jealous by any chance?

ARTHUR: I am not jealous.

ALA: First he's brutal. Then he's jealous. You ought to be ashamed of yourself.

ARTHUR (*furious, face to face with* ALA): Go on then. Undress! I'm not stopping you.

ALA: I don't feel like it anymore.

ARTHUR: Suit yourself.

ALA (*retreating*): I've changed my mind.

ARTHUR (*following her*): Oh, you don't feel like it anymore? Tell me, why don't you want to anymore! Tell me why you wanted to before.

ALA: My God, what a lunatic!

ARTHUR (*seizes her by the arm*): Why?

ALA: I don't know.

ARTHUR: Tell me!

ALA: What should I say? I don't know, I just don't know. Let me go.

ARTHUR (*letting her go*): You know perfectly well. It's because you only pretend to like all this absence of rules, this debauchery, this promiscuity.

ALA: Oh, I only pretend, do I?

ARTHUR: Of course. You really hate it, because it's not to your advantage. This lack of forms and norms cuts down your freedom of choice. There's nothing left for you to do but take off your clothes and put them back on again.

ALA: That's not true.

ARTHUR: Then why this sudden modesty?

Pause.

ALA: Now you're being logical. You just said that logic was nonsense.

ARTHUR: I said that?

ALA: Yes, only a minute ago. I heard you.

ARTHUR (*disgruntled*): You must have heard wrong.

ALA: I heard you quite clearly.

ARTHUR: Well, let's not bicker. But I still don't believe you. I'm convinced that the convention of unconventionality goes against your grain. You didn't make it up.

ALA: Who did then?

ARTHUR: Men! You only pretend to like it. And now you're stuck with it, and nobody likes to admit he's just following the herd.

ALA: But if I don't like it why should I go along with it?

ARTHUR: For fear of losing your attractiveness. To keep up with the fashion. Admit it!

ALA: No.

ARTHUR: No? All right. At least you admit there's something to admit. Come on. Why all these lies? Can't you see that important issues are at stake? I simply refuse to believe that you want to go to bed with every man in the world. Wanting to attract them is something else again. You want to be able to choose for yourself. But how can a woman choose when there are no conventions? Tell me that.

ALA: I'm free. I know exactly what I want.

ARTHUR: But you're weak by nature. What chance do you have when you're all alone with a strange man who's stronger than you and there's no convention to protect you? Let's assume, for instance, that you don't care for me. If Eddie hadn't butted in, you'd have been sunk, because I'm the stronger.

ALA: I could always take up judo.

ARTHUR: You take everything so literally. Can't you women ever understand a general idea?

ALA: Lots of girls study judo. I'd have you begging for mercy.

ARTHUR: Excellent. You're getting there. You're coming around. Don't you see? Why does it have to be judo when conventions are quite effective? I'd be kneeling at your feet with a bouquet in my hand begging you to take pity on me, to grant me a ray of hope. Behind a solid wall of conventions, without any wrestling, without even getting your hair mussed, you'd have me at your mercy. Wouldn't that be better than judo?

ALA: You really mean it? Down on your knees?

ARTHUR: Certainly.

ALA: Okay. Go ahead.

ARTHUR: Go ahead and what?

ALA: Down on your knees!

ARTHUR: Impossible.

ALA (*disappointed*): Why?

ARTHUR: Because there are no conventions left. Now do you see what a fix you're in?

ALA: Isn't there anything we can do about it?

ARTHUR: Yes.

ALA: What?

ARTHUR: Establish new conventions or bring back the old ones. And that's exactly what I'm going to do—with your help. Everything's prepared. All I need is your help.

ALA: Great! And you'll really get down on your knees?

ARTHUR: I will.

ALA: All right. Now what can I do to help?

ARTHUR: Marry me. That's the first step. No more promiscuity, no more *dolce vita*. A real marriage. Not just dropping into city hall between breakfast and lunch. A genuine old-fashioned wedding with an organ playing and bridesmaids marching down the aisle. I'm especially counting on the procession. It will take them by surprise. That's the whole idea. And, from then on, they won't have time to think, to organize resistance and spread defeatism. It's the first shot that counts. Catching them off guard like that, we can force them to accept conventions they'll never break out of again. It's going to be the kind of wedding they'll have to take part in, and on my terms. I'll turn them into a bridal procession, and at long last my father will be forced to button his fly. What do you say?

ALA: And I'll get to wear a white wedding gown?

ARTHUR: White as snow. Everything strictly according to the rules. And at the same time you'll be helping all the women in the world. The rebirth of convention will set them free. What used to be the first rule of every encounter between a man and a woman? Conversation. A man couldn't get what he wanted just by making inarticulate sounds. He couldn't just grunt, he had to talk. And while he was talking, you—the woman—sat there demurely, sizing your opponent up. You let him talk and he showed his hand. Listening serenely, you drew up your own order of battle. Observing his tactics, you planned your own accordingly. Free to maneuver, you were always in command of the situation. You had time to think before coming to a decision and you could drag things out as long as you wanted. Even if he gnashed his teeth and secretly wished you in the bottom of hell, you knew he would never dare hit you. Up to the very last minute you could move freely, securely, triumphantly. Once you were engaged, you were safe, and even then traditional avenues of escape were open to you. Such were the blessings of conversation! But nowadays? Nowadays a man doesn't even have to introduce himself—and you will admit it's handy to know who a man is and what he does for a living.

EDDIE *tiptoes from the kitchen door to the door right. As he disappears in the doorway,* ARTHUR *sees him and goes after him.*

ALA: Was somebody listening?
ARTHUR (*coming back*): No.
ALA: I had the feeling there was.
ARTHUR: Let's settle this matter once and for all. Do you consent?
ALA: I don't know yet.
ARTHUR: You don't know? You mean I haven't convinced you?
ALA: Yes.

ARTHUR: Yes? Then you consent?

ALA: No . . .

ARTHUR: Yes or no?

ALA: I've got to think about it.

ARTHUR: But what is there to think about? It's as plain as day. I've got to rebuild a world, and for that I must have a wedding. It's perfectly simple. What don't you understand?

ALA: The whole thing, I guess.

ARTHUR: What do you mean?

ALA: Wait . . . Give me time.

ARTHUR: No, I can't wait. There just isn't time. I'll stay here while you go think it over. When you've made up your mind, come back and give me your answer. It's sure to be yes. I've explained everything.

ALA: And you really have nothing else to say? There's really nothing else you want to tell me?

ARTHUR: Run along now. I'll see you later.

ALA: You're throwing me out?

ARTHUR: No, I have a little private business to attend to.

ALA: Can't I stay?

ARTHUR: No. This is a family matter.

ALA: All right. Then I'll have my little secrets too. Just wait. You'll see.

ARTHUR (*impatiently*): Yes, yes, but run along now. Remember, I'll be waiting for you here.

> ALA *goes out right.* ARTHUR *listens at the door left rear, and then goes to the door in the corridor. He knocks softly.*

STOMIL'S VOICE: Who's there?

ARTHUR (*rather softly*): Me. Arthur.

STOMIL: What do you want?

ARTHUR: Father, I've got to talk to you.

STOMIL: At this time of night? I'm busy. Come back tomorrow.

ARTHUR: It's urgent.

Pause.

STOMIL: But I've already told you, I'm busy. You can speak to me tomorrow.

ARTHUR *tries the door and sees that it is locked. He shoves with his shoulder.* STOMIL *opens. He is in pajamas as usual.*

Are you mad? What's going on?

ARTHUR (*in an ominous whisper*): Not so loud, Father.

STOMIL (*whispering, too, in spite of himself*): Why aren't you in bed?

ARTHUR: I can't sleep. It's time to take action.

STOMIL: In that case, good night.

He starts for his room. ARTHUR *holds him back.*

ARTHUR: I only wanted to ask you, Father, doesn't it bother you?

STOMIL: What?

ARTHUR: This thing with Eddie.

STOMIL: Eddie? Oh yes, I remember the man.

ARTHUR: What do you think of him?

STOMIL: He's amusing.

ARTHUR: Amusing? He's repulsive.

STOMIL: Oh I wouldn't say that. Eddie's an unusual type. A very modern, very authentic type.

ARTHUR: Is that all you have to say about him?

STOMIL: You see, our trouble is that we're still too conscious, too cerebral. Enslaved by centuries of culture.

Of course we've been doing our best to throw culture off, but we're still a long way from nature. But Eddie's lucky. He was born with what the rest of us can acquire only by art and effort. He interests me as an artist. I admire him the way a painter admires a landscape.

ARTHUR: Some landscape!

STOMIL: But don't you know there's been a complete revolution in aesthetics and morality. You keep making me remind you of things that ought to be self-evident. If Eddie shocks us now and then, it's because we're decadent. Sometimes I can't help feeling guilty toward Eddie. But I fight it down. We've got to get rid of these atavistic attitudes.

ARTHUR: And that's all you have to say?

STOMIL: I've been perfectly frank with you.

ARTHUR: Then I'll have to start all over again. Why do you tolerate him in your house?

STOMIL: Why not? He enriches our environment, he gives it a new tone, he adds a dash of authenticity. He even stimulates my imagination. We artists need an exotic touch now and then.

ARTHUR: Then you really don't know?

STOMIL: No, I don't know a thing.

ARTHUR: You're lying. You know perfectly well.

STOMIL: I repeat—I don't know. I don't want to know.

ARTHUR: He sleeps with Mother.

STOMIL *starts pacing.*

What do you say to that?

STOMIL: My dear boy. Let's assume what you say is true. Sexual freedom is the cornerstone of human freedom. What do *you* say to that?

ARTHUR: But it's the truth! They *do* sleep together!

STOMIL: I said we'd assume it's true. What follows? Nothing.

ARTHUR: Then you insist on treating it as an abstract hypothesis?

STOMIL: Why not? I'm a modern man. On the intellectual plane we can envisage any hypothesis, even the most ticklish. Without such hypotheses human thought would mark time. So do speak freely. I trust we can discuss this business without prudery. Now, what's your opinion?

ARTHUR: My opinion? I haven't got any opinion and I refuse to treat this matter as a theoretical exercise. This isn't a philosophical problem. It's the naked truth. Can't you see that? It's life. They've put horns on you. Long ones! And arguing isn't going to make them go away.

STOMIL: Horns! Horns! Horns are a primitive image, not an instrument of analysis. (*Nervously.*) Let's not descend to that low level.

ARTHUR: Father, you're a cuckold.

STOMIL: Hold your tongue. I forbid you to talk to me like that.

ARTHUR: You can't stop me. You're a cuckold.

STOMIL: I don't believe it.

ARTHUR: Ha! Now I've got you where I want you. Want me to prove it? Open that door. (*He points to the door left rear.*)

STOMIL: No!

ARTHUR: Are you afraid? Of course it's easier to perform theatrical experiments. When it comes to experiments you're a giant. In real life you're a midget.

STOMIL: Me?

ARTHUR: A hero in pajamas! A pint-sized Agamemnon!

STOMIL: I'll show you. You say they're in there?

ARTHUR: Look for yourself.

STOMIL: I'll show them. I'll show you. I'll show the whole lot of you! (*He runs to the door, stops.*) Or you know what I'll do? I'll take care of this whole thing tomorrow. (*He turns around.*)

ARTHUR (*barring the way*): No you won't. You're going in there right now.

STOMIL: Tomorrow! Or by mail. A letter. What do you say?

ARTHUR: Phony!

STOMIL: What did you say?

> ARTHUR *makes horns on his forehead and laughs sardonically.*

All right then. Here I go!

ARTHUR (*stops him*): Just a second.

STOMIL (*with a martial air*): Let me at them.

ARTHUR: You'd better take this.

> *He takes the revolver which* STOMIL *had left on the catafalque in Act One and gives it to his father.*

STOMIL: What's that?

ARTHUR: You can't go in there bare-handed.

> *Pause.*

STOMIL (*calmly*): Now I see through you.

ARTHUR (*pushing him toward the door*): Get in there! There's not a minute to lose.

STOMIL (*tearing himself loose*): Now I understand. You want a tragedy!

ARTHUR (*retreating*): A tragedy? What do you mean?

STOMIL: So that's what you're after, you dim little runt of a brainstorm, you . . .

ARTHUR: What are you trying . . .

STOMIL (*throwing the revolver on the table*): You want me to kill him? And then her? And then myself? Right?

ARTHUR: Of course not. I was only joking. I just thought that in case Eddie . . . he might do anything.

STOMIL: You'd love that, wouldn't you! The injured husband wiping out his shame in blood. Where do you *get* such ideas? From romantic novels?

ARTHUR: Father, you know I never . . .

STOMIL: I always knew the younger generation cared more about ideas than life, but I never expected my own son to sacrifice his father to an idea. Sit down!

ARTHUR *sits down obediently.*

That's it. Now we'll have a little talk. You want to bring back the old values. What for? Well, never mind that. That's your business. I've let you talk, I've heard you out, but now you're going just a bit too far. How fiendishly clever! So you need a tragedy! Tragedy has always been the most perfect expression of a society with established values. So you needed a tragedy and thought you'd drag me into it. Instead of the art form—which demands time and effort—you wanted the thing itself. Or, never mind if somebody's killed, never mind if your own father goes off to prison. No, all you care about is your idea. Do you want to know what I think of you? A formalist. A vulgar formalist. That's what you are. Your father and mother mean nothing to you. We can all die as long as form wins out. And the worst of it is that you don't even care about yourself. You're a fanatic!

ARTHUR: Maybe my motives aren't as formal as you think.

STOMIL: You dislike Eddie?

ARTHUR: I hate him.

STOMIL: Why? Eddie is necessity. He's the pure truth we've
 been searching for so long because we always thought
 it was somewhere else. Eddie is a fact. You can't hate
 facts. You've got to accept them.

ARTHUR: What do you want me to do, hug him?

STOMIL: Good Lord! You talk like a petulant child. I can
 only see one explanation. Maybe you've got an
 Oedipus.

ARTHUR: A what?

STOMIL: An Oedipus complex. Have you consulted an
 analyst?

ARTHUR: No. Mother's wonderful, but that's not it.

STOMIL: Too bad. Then at least we'd know where we were at.
 Anything is better than sheer lunacy. I guess you're
 just a formalist.

ARTHUR: I am not.

STOMIL: Oh yes you are. And an insufferable and dangerous
 one at that.

ARTHUR: It may look that way to you, but the truth is that
 I . . . I just can't go on like this. I can't live with you
 people.

STOMIL: I see. That's more like it. In other words, you're
 an egoist.

ARTHUR: Call it whatever you like. That's the way I am,
 that's all.

STOMIL: But suppose you succeeded in making me kill him,
 in packing me off to prison for life, what good would
 that do you?

ARTHUR: Something would be accomplished. Something
 tragic. You're right. Please forgive me. Tragedy is a
 form so vast and powerful that reality can never escape
 its grip.

STOMIL: You poor devil. You really believe that? Don't

you realize that tragedy isn't possible anymore? Reality erodes all forms and that goes for tragedy too. Suppose I actually killed him. What would be the good of it?

ARTHUR: It would be something irrevocable, masterful, classical.

STOMIL: Not for a minute. It would be a farce. In our time only farce is possible. A corpse won't change anything. Why can't you face facts? Actually, a farce can be very nice too.

ARTHUR: Not for me.

STOMIL: Lord, you can be stubborn!

ARTHUR: I can't help it. I've got to find a way out.

STOMIL: Regardless of reality?

ARTHUR: Yes. At any cost.

STOMIL: That's not so easy. I'd like to help you, but I don't see how.

ARTHUR: Couldn't we give it a try?

STOMIL: Give what a try?

ARTHUR (*pointing to the door left rear*): With them.

STOMIL: You still have illusions?

ARTHUR: Even if you're right about farce . . . (*Gradually he resumes his aggressiveness.*) It's only because you people are such cowards. You complain, but you're stuck in a farce because no one has the courage to rebel. Why can't you free yourself by one act of sheer violence? You're so logical, so analytical, you see everything in the abstract. Instead of changing anything, you make diagrams. You've come a long way, but what have you actually done? Sat in a chair and discussed. But this situation calls for action. If tragedy has become extinct it's only because you don't believe in it. You and your damned compromises.

STOMIL: But why should we believe in tragedy? Come here,

son. I want to tell you something. All right. Eleanor is unfaithful to me with Eddie. What's so bad about that?

ARTHUR: But, Father, don't you know?

STOMIL: So help me, when you come right down to it, I don't. Maybe you can explain.

ARTHUR: I've never been in such a situation . . .

STOMIL: Try.

ARTHUR: It's obvious . . . Let me think . . .

STOMIL: Think away. Actually, I'd be delighted if you could convince me.

ARTHUR: Really?

STOMIL: To tell you the truth, I don't much care for this kind of thing either. In fact, I detest it. Only the more I think about it, the less I know why.

ARTHUR: So if I could convince you . . .

STOMIL: . . . I'd be very grateful.

ARTHUR: And you'd . . .

STOMIL: Go in and make a scene they'd remember as long as they lived. But I need a rational justification.

ARTHUR: Then you'd go in? Without being pushed?

STOMIL: I'd be delighted to. I've had it in for that bastard a long time. Believe it or not, nothing would please me doesn't tell me why.

more than to settle his hash. Except that my reason

ARTHUR: Father, let me hug you.

They hug each other.

To hell with reason!

STOMIL: But what can we do? It won't let go of us. You were talking about compromise. It's reason that makes us compromise.

ARTHUR: Well, then, Father, shall we give it a try? What

have we got to lose? If the worst comes to the worst, you'll shoot him.

STOMIL: Think so? If I could only be sure.

ARTHUR: Certainty comes later. The main thing now is to make up your mind.

STOMIL: Hm. Maybe you're right.

ARTHUR: I know I'm right. You'll see. We'll have our tragedy!

STOMIL: You've given me back my strength. The enthusiasm of youth untrammeled by the skepticism of the times. Ah, youth, youth!

ARTHUR: Shall we go in?

STOMIL: Yes. With you beside me, I feel better.

They stand up.

ARTHUR: Just one more thing. Give up those experiments of yours, will you? They only speed up the process of disintegration.

STOMIL: Well, but what can we do? Tragedy impossible, farce a bore—what's left but experiments?

ARTHUR: They only make things worse. Give them up, Father.

STOMIL: I don't know . . .

ARTHUR: Promise.

STOMIL: Later. Now we go in.

ARTHUR *puts the revolver back into Stomil's hand.*

ARTHUR: I'll wait here. If you need any help, just shout.

STOMIL: That won't be necessary. If anybody yells, it'll be him, not me.

ARTHUR: Father, I've always had confidence in you.

STOMIL: With good reason, my boy. I was the best shot in my regiment. Farewell! (*He goes to the door right rear.*)

ARTHUR: No, that's the kitchen.

STOMIL (*irresolute*): I could use a drink.

ARTHUR: Later. When it's all over. No time now.

STOMIL: Right! I'll kill him on the spot. (*He goes to the left-hand door, puts his hand on the knob.*) That scoundrel! Now he's going to pay!

He enters the room cautiously, closes the door behind him. ARTHUR *waits tensely. Total silence.* ARTHUR *paces nervously back and forth. Grows more and more impatient. Looks at his watch. Finally he makes a decision and flings both wings of the door open, so that the whole room can be seen. Under a bright, low-hanging lamp* ELEANOR, EDDIE, EUGENIA *and* STOMIL *are sitting at a round table, playing cards.*

ARTHUR: What's Eddie doing here? Why isn't Eddie . . . ?

STOMIL: Shhh! Take it easy, boy!

ELEANOR: Oh, it's you, Arthur? Are you still up?

EUGENIA: I told you he'd find us. He sticks his nose into everything.

ARTHUR: Father! . . . You . . . with them!

STOMIL: That's how it worked out . . . It's not *my* fault.

ELEANOR: Stomil turned up just in time. We needed a fourth.

ARTHUR: Father, how could you!

STOMIL: I told you it would end in a farce.

EDDIE: Your play, Mr. Stomil. What you got?

STOML: Here you are. (*To* ARTHUR.) A harmless pastime. You see the situation. What could I do?

ARTHUR: But, Father, you promised!

STOMIL: I promised nothing. We'll just have to wait.

ELEANOR: Instead of talking so much, would you please put your mind on the game, Stomil?

ARTHUR: For shame!

EUGENIA (*throws down her cards*): I simply can't play under these conditions. Can't anybody throw this little twerp out of here?

EDDIE: Easy, Grandma. Take it easy.

ELEANOR: Arthur, you ought to be ashamed, upsetting your grandmother like this.

EUGENIA: I told you we should lock the door. He's always looking for some way to pester me. You'll see. He'll put me back up on the catafalque!

ELEANOR: Oh, no he won't! We've got to finish this rubber first.

ARTHUR (*pounding the table with his fist*): Stop it!

ELEANOR: But we've just started.

EDDIE: You'd better listen to your mother. She's right. Look at the score cards, they're practically blank.

ARTHUR (*tearing the cards out of their hands*): Now you listen to me! I've got something to tell you. Now! This minute!

STOMIL: But Arthur, that was strictly between the two of us. Don't shout it from the rooftops.

ARTHUR: I pleaded with you. You wouldn't listen. Now I'm going to use force. Stop the game!

ELEANOR: What's going on?

EDDIE: What's got into you anyway? If I were your father, know what I'd do? I'd give you a good hiding.

ARTHUR: You shut up. (*Calmly but firmly.*) Father, the revolver.

EDDIE: A guy can still make a joke, can't he?

ELEANOR: A revolver? For God's sake, Stomil, don't give it to him. Talk to him. Do *something*. After all, you're his father.

STOMIL (*trying to take a severe tone*): Now see here,

Arthur, you're not a child. I'm sorry to have to speak to you like this, but . . .

ARTHUR *takes the revolver from Stomil's pajama pocket. All jump up.*

EUGENIA: He's gone mad. Stomil, why on earth did you make this child? Criminal negligence—that's what I call it.

EDDIE: Look here, Mr. Arthur . . .

ARTHUR: Silence! Into the living room, everybody.

One after another they go to the center of the stage. ARTHUR *remains standing at the door. As* STOMIL *passes him.*

I'll talk to you later.

STOMIL: What's wrong? I did my best.

ARTHUR: Your best!

EUGENIA *sits down on the sofa,* ELEANOR *in an armchair.* EDDIE *stands in the corner, takes a comb from his back pocket and runs it nervously through his hair.*

STOMIL (*facing* ELEANOR, *raises his arms*): I did everything I could to quiet him down. You saw me . . .

ELEANOR: Idiot. And you call yourself a father. Oh, if I were only a man!

STOMIL: That's easier said than done.

EUGENE *runs in.*

EUGENE (*to* ARTHUR): Has it started yet?

ARTHUR: Not yet. I'm still waiting for an answer.

EUGENE: I thought it had started. I heard a noise and I came running.

ARTHUR: That's all right. I'm glad you've come. Stay here and keep an eye on them. I'll be back in a second.

He gives him the revolver.

EUGENE: Yes, sir.

ELEANOR: Am I dreaming?

ARTHUR (*to* EUGENE): Don't let anybody make a move.

EUGENE: Yes, sir.

ELEANOR: Have you both gone mad?

ARTHUR: If anybody does move, shoot to kill. Understand?

EUGENE: Yes, sir.

ELEANOR: It's a plot! Mama, your brother's a gangster!

EUGENIA: Eugene, do put that thing away. People don't play cowboys at your age. (*She starts to stand up.*)

EUGENE: Stay where you are!

EUGENIA (*astonished*): Eugene, it's me—your sister Eugenia.

EUGENE: When I'm on duty, I have no sister.

EUGENIA: What duty? Don't be a fool.

EUGENE: I have enlisted in the service of an ideal!

ARTHUR: Splendid. I see I can rely on you. I'm going to leave you for a moment.

STOMIL: But, Arthur, can't you tell me, at least, what's going on? I thought we'd just become friends.

ARTHUR: I'll tell you everything in due time.

He goes out. EUGENE *sits down with his back to the wall, holding his revolver in readiness. He aims it vaguely but menacingly at each in turn.*

ELEANOR (*after a pause*): So that's it . . . Eugene, you've betrayed us.

EUGENE: Silence! (*Then justifying himself.*) That's not true I haven't betrayed anybody.

ARTHUR'S VOICE (*off*): Ala! Ala!

ELEANOR: You've betrayed your generation.

EUGENE: No, you're the traitors. You've all betrayed our good old days. I'm the only one who hasn't.

ARTHUR'S VOICE (*off*): Ala! Ala!

ELEANOR: All you are is the tool of a mad pack of young zealots. With a missionary complex. You think you're so clever. They'll use you and then kick you out like a dog.

EUGENE: We'll see who uses whom. I've been waiting a long time for someone like Arthur to come along.

ELEANOR: Now at least you've shown who you really are. All these years you've been wearing a mask, you hypocrite.

EUGENE: Yes, I have. And all these years I've suffered. I hated you for your degradation but I kept quiet because I had to, because you were the stronger. Now at last I can tell you what I think of you! What a pleasure!

ELEANOR: What are you going to do to us?

EUGENE: We're going to give you back your dignity. We're going to turn you degenerates back into human beings with decent principles—that's what we're going to do.

ELEANOR: By force?

EUGENE: If we can't do it any other way, yes.

STOMIL: This is a counter-reformation.

EUGENE: But for you it's salvation.

STOMIL: Salvation? From what?

EUGENE: From your damnable, diabolical freedom.

ARTHUR (*enters*): Uncle!

EUGENE: Sir?

ARTHUR: She's gone.

EUGENE: Look for her. She must be somewhere.

ARTHUR: Yes. She's got to be. I'm still waiting for her answer.

EUGENE: What? You mean she hasn't consented yet?

ARTHUR: She's got to. Everything else is ready now. She can't leave me in the lurch at a moment like this.

EUGENE: I don't mean to criticize you, Arthur, but haven't you rushed things a bit? I mean, shouldn't you have made sure of *her* before starting in on (*he points to the others with his pistol barrel*) these people?

ARTHUR: The time was ripe. I couldn't put it off.

EUGENE: Well, that's how it is with a *coup d'état*. Always some unforeseeable factor. Still, we can't back out now.

ARTHUR: Who could have dreamed of such a thing? I was so sure I had convinced her. (*He calls.*) Ala, Ala! (*Irritably.*) All because of some dumb cousin. Incredible! (*He calls.*) Ala, Ala.

EUGENE: Women have been the ruin of kingdoms and empires.

ALA (*enters*): Gosh, are you all still up?

ARTHUR (*reproachfully*): At last! I've been looking all over for you.

ALA: What's going on? Uncle with a gun? Is it real? Is Uncle real?

ARTHUR: That's none of your business. Where have you been?

ALA: Out for a walk. Anything wrong with that?

EUGENE: Yes! At this solemn hour, there is.

ARTHUR: Steady, Uncle. You're on duty, remember. (*To ALA.*) Well?

ALA: Well, what? It's a lovely night.

ARTHUR: I wasn't asking about the weather. Do you consent?

ALA: I think I need a little more time, Arthur.

ARTHUR: I need an answer immediately. You've had plenty of time.

Pause.

ALA: Yes.

EUGENE: Hurrah!

ARTHUR: Thank God! Now we can start!

He gives ALA *his arm and leads her to the sofa where* EUGENIA *is sitting.*

Grandmother, your blessing.

EUGENIA (*starts up from the sofa in a fright*): Oh, leave me alone. I haven't done anything to you.

ARTHUR: But Grandmother, everything's changed now. I'm going to marry Ala. Give us your blessing.

EUGENE (*to the others*): On your feet, everybody! Can't you see this is a solemn occasion?

ELEANOR: My goodness, is Arthur going to get married?

STOMIL: Is that any reason to make such a fuss?

EUGENIA: Get that boy out of here! He's going to torture me again.

ARTHUR (*menacingly*): Grandmother, your blessing.

STOMIL: A tasteless joke. It's gone on long enough now.

EUGENE (*triumphantly*): The jokes are over now. You've been having your jokes for fifty years. Stomil, button your pajamas immediately! Your son has just plighted his troth. The day of the wide-open fly is past. Bless them, Eugenia.

EUGENIA: What should I do, Eleanor?

ELEANOR: Give them your blessing if it means so much to them.

EUGENIA: Can't they do without it? It makes me feel so old.

EUGENE: A good old-fashioned engagement. Give them your blessing, or I'll shoot. I'm going to count to three. One . . .

STOMIL: This is incredible. If a man can't be comfortable in his own house . . . (*He tries to button his pajamas.*)

EUGENE: Two . . .

EUGENIA (*lays her hand on the heads of* ALA *and* ARTHUR): My blessing upon you, dear children . . . and now go to hell!

EUGENE (*moved*): Just like old times.

ARTHUR (*stands up and kisses Eugenia's hand*): We thank you, Grandmother.

EUGENE: Stomil has buttoned his fly! A whole new era has begun!

STOMIL: Eleanor! You're crying?

ELEANOR (*sobbing with emotion*): Forgive me . . . But Arthur's getting engaged . . . and after all he is our son . . . I know I'm being terribly old-fashioned, but it's so moving. Forgive me.

STOMIL: Oh, do what you want, all of you! (*He runs out of the room in a rage.*)

EDDIE: If you'll permit me, on this joyous occasion I would like to wish the young couple all the best for the days to come and especially . . .

Holds out his hand to ARTHUR.

ARTHUR (*not taking his hand*): You! To the kitchen!

He points dramatically to the kitchen door. EDDIE *saunters out.*

And stay there until you're called.

EUGENE: To the kitchen.

ELEANOR (*in tears*): When's the wedding?

ARTHUR: Tomorrow.

EUGENE: Hurray! We've won!

ACT THREE

Daylight. The same room, but with no trace now of the former disorder: a conventional middle-class living room of about fifty years ago. None of the previous confusion and blurred contours. The draperies which had been lying about, giving the impression of an unmade bed, are now hung in orderly fashion. The catafalque is still in its old place—the curtain in front of the alcove is drawn back— but it is covered with napkins and knicknacks, so that it looks like a buffet.

On stage ELEANOR, EUGENIA, STOMIL, *and* EUGENE. EUGENIA *is sitting on the sofa in the middle of the room. She is wearing a bonnet and a dark gray or brown dress buttoned up to the neck and adorned with lace cuffs and ruching. She has a lorgnette which she frequently raises to her eyes. To her right sits* ELEANOR *with her hair done up in a chignon; she is wearing earrings and a striped violet or burgundy-colored dress gathered at the waist. Both sit bolt upright, immobile, their hands on their knees. Beside them stands* STOMIL, *his hair combed, pomaded and parted in the middle. His stiff collar forces him to stretch his head as though looking into the distance. He is wearing a brown suit that is obviously too tight for him, and white spats. He is resting one hand on a little round table on which stands a vase with flowers; the other is braced on his hip. One foot is balanced nonchalantly on the tip of his shoe. In front of the group near the proscenium, a large camera on a tripod, covered with black velvet. Behind the camera stands*

EUGENE. *He is still wearing his black swallowtail coat but his khaki shorts have been replaced by long black trousers with pin stripes. A red carnation in his buttonhole. In front of him on the floor, his top hat, white gloves and a cane with a silver knob. He fusses with the camera while the others hold their pose.* EUGENIA *says "Ah . . . ah" several times and sneezes loudly.*

EUGENE: Don't move!

EUGENIA: I can't help it. It's the moth balls.

EUGENE: Hold it!

> STOMIL *removes his hand from his hip and scratches his chest.*

Stomil, your hand.

STOMIL: But I'm itching all over.

ELEANOR: Why should you be itching?

STOMIL: Moths.

ELEANOR: Moths! (*She jumps up and runs across the stage, chasing moths, occasionally clapping her hands.*)

EUGENE: At this rate we'll never get a picture. Sit down, Eleanor.

ELEANOR (*reproachfully*): The moths come from Mama.

EUGENIA: They do not. They come out of this old rag.

EUGENE: Let's not quarrel. They come from the attic.

EDDIE (*enters dressed as a valet, in a crimson vest with black stripes*): You called, Madame?

ELEANOR (*stops clapping her hands*): What? What is it now? Oh yes. My salts, Edward!

EDDIE: Salts, Madame?

ELEANOR: Those smelling salts . . . you know . . .

EDDIE: Certainly, Madame. (*He goes out.*)

STOMIL (*looking after him*): I must admit it's a relief to see that fellow put in his place.

EUGENE: You haven't seen anything yet. Everything's going splendidly. You won't regret a thing.

STOMIL (*tries to loosen his collar*): If only this collar weren't so damn tight!

EUGENE: That's the price you've got to pay for having Eddie wait on you. Everything has its price.

STOMIL: And my experiments? Will I have to give them up?

EUGENE: I couldn't say. Arthur hasn't announced his decision on that point yet.

STOMIL: Maybe he'll let me go on with them. He hasn't said anything?

EUGENE: There hasn't been time. He went out early this morning.

STOMIL: Perhaps you could put in a good word for me, Uncle?

EUGENE (*patronizingly*): I'll speak to him when the opportunity arises.

STOMIL: At least once a week. After all these years I can't just suddenly stop. You ought to realize that.

EUGENE: That will depend entirely on your conduct, Stomil.

STOMIL: But I'm on your side. What more do you want? I'm even putting up with this collar. (*He tries again to loosen it.*)

EUGENE: Well, I can't promise.

EDDIE *enters with a tray on which a bottle of vodka is very much in evidence.*

What is that?

EDDIE: The salts for Madame, sir.

EUGENE (*menacingly*): Eleanor, what is the meaning of this?

ELEANOR: I can't imagine. (*To* EDDIE.) I asked for my smelling salts.

EDDIE: Madame no longer drinks?

ELEANOR: Take it away immediately!

EUGENIA: Why? As long as he's brought it . . . I don't feel too well.

EDDIE: As you wish, Madame.

He goes out. On the way he takes a good swig from the bottle. Only EUGENIA, *looking after him longingly, notices.*

EUGENE: Don't let it happen again!

EUGENIA: God, am I bored!

EUGENE: Back to your places!

ELEANOR, STOMIL *and* EUGENIA *sit up and freeze as at the beginning of the act.* EUGENE *ducks under the velvet cloth, the ticking of the timer is heard.* EUGENE *reaches quickly for his stick, top hat and gloves, and takes a stance beside* EUGENIA. *The ticking stops. Relieved, they all relax.*

STOMIL: Can't I unbutton these buttons for just a second?

EUGENE: Certainly not! The wedding is at twelve!

STOMIL: I seem to have put on weight. The last time I wore these things was forty years ago.

EUGENE: You have only your experiments to blame for that. Experimental art pays so well these days.

STOMIL: That's not my fault, is it?

ELEANOR: When will that picture be ready? I think I blinked. I know I'm going to look simply awful.

EUGENE: Don't worry. The camera hasn't worked for years.

ELEANOR: What? Then why take the picture?

EUGENE: It's the principle of the thing. It's a tradition.

STOMIL: You begrudge me my innocent experiments but is an old-fashioned broken-down camera any better? You know what I think of your counterrevolution? It's a fiasco.

EUGENE: Watch your tongue.

STOMIL: I bow to superior force, but I can still say what I think.

ELEANOR (*to* EUGENIA): What do you say, Mother?

EUGENIA: I say we're in one hell of a mess and this is only the beginning.

EUGENE: It can't be helped. Our first job is to create the form. The content comes later.

STOMIL: You're making a colossal mistake, Eugene. Formalism will never free you from chaos. You'd be better off if you could just accept the spirit of the times.

EUGENE: That's enough out of you. Defeatism will not be tolerated!

STOMIL: All right, all right. I can still have an opinion, can't I?

EUGENE: Of course. As long as it agrees with ours.

ELEANOR: Listen!

Bells are heard in the distance.

STOMIL: Bells!

EUGENE: Wedding bells.

ALA *enters. She is wearing a wedding dress with a long veil.* STOMIL *kisses her hand.*

STOMIL: Ah, here comes our dear little bride!

ELEANOR: Oh, Ala, it's so becoming!

EUGENIA: My dear child!

ALA: Isn't Arthur back yet?

EUGENE: We're expecting him any minute. He had a few final formalities to attend to.

ALA: These damned formalities.

EUGENE: But the spirit of life can't run around naked. It must always be dressed with taste and care. You mean Arthur hasn't discussed that point with you yet?

ALA: For hours on end.

EUGENE: And rightly so. Someday you'll understand and be grateful to him.

ALA: Oh, stop making such an ass of yourself, Uncle.

ELEANOR: You mustn't talk like that, Ala dear. Today is your wedding day and no time for family quarrels. There'll be plenty of time for that later.

EUGENE: Don't worry. No offense. I quite understand.

ALA: So old and so stupid. I can understand it in Arthur. But you, Uncle . . .

ELEANOR: Ala!

STOMIL: He had it coming.

ELEANOR: Forgive her, Eugene. She's so excited she doesn't know what she's saying. After all, this is a big day in her life. I remember the day I was married to Stomil . . .

EUGENE: I can tell when I'm not wanted. But don't delude yourselves. You can laugh at me as much as you like but childish insults won't change a thing. Stomil, come with me. I have a proposition to make to you.

STOMIL: All right. Just don't try to brainwash me!

They go out.

ELEANOR: Mama, you might go for a stroll too.

EUGENIA: Anything you say. It's all the same to me. Either way I'll be bored to death. (*She goes out.*)

ELEANOR: There. Now we can talk. Tell me, what's happened?

ALA: Nothing.

ELEANOR: Something's bothering you. I can see that.

ALA: Nothing's bothering me. This veil doesn't fall quite right. Help me with it, will you, Mother?

ELEANOR: Of course. But you don't have to take that tone with me. With the others it's different. They're such fools.

ALA (*sits down at the mirror; the bells are still ringing*): Why do you all despise each other?

ELEANOR: I don't know. Maybe because we have no reason to respect each other.

ALA: Yourselves or each other?

ELEANOR: It comes to the same thing. Shall I fix your hair?

ALA: It's got to be done all over again.

She takes off her veil. ELEANOR *combs her hair.*

Are you happy, Mother?

ELEANOR: I beg your pardon?

ALA: I asked if you were happy. What's so funny about that?

ELEANOR: It's a very indiscreet question.

ALA: Why? Is it a disgrace to be happy?

ELEANOR: No, I wouldn't say that.

ALA: Then you're not very happy, are you? Because you're ashamed. People are always ashamed about not being happy. It's like having pimples or not doing your homework. It makes them feel guilty, almost criminal.

ELEANOR: "It is the right and duty of all to be happy, now that the new era has set us free." Stomil taught me that.

ALA: Oh. So that's why everybody's so ashamed nowadays. But how do *you* feel about it?

ELEANOR: I've always done as much as I could.

ALA: To make Stomil happy?

ELEANOR: No. Myself. That's the way he wanted it.

ALA: Then in a way it was for him?

ELEANOR: Of course it was for him. Oh, if you'd only known him when he was young . . .

ALA: It's not right yet on this side. Does he know?

ELEANOR: What?

ALA: Don't be like that. I'm not a baby. Your affair with Eddie.

ELEANOR: Of course he knows.

ALA: And what does he say?

ELEANOR: Nothing, unfortunately. He pretends not to notice.

ALA: That's bad.

EDDIE *comes in with a white tablecloth.*

EDDIE: May I set the table now?

ELEANOR: Sure, Eddie. (*She corrects herself.*) Yes, Edward, you may set the table.

EDDIE: Yes, Madame. (*He lays the cloth on the table and takes the camera out with him.*)

ALA: What do you see in him?

ELEANOR: Oh, he's just so simple . . . like life itself. He can be rough, of course, but that's the secret of his charm. A man without complexes—it's so refreshing. He just wants what he wants. Wonderful. And the way he sits —nothing unusual about it, but it's real, honest-to-goodness sitting. And when he eats, when he drinks! His stomach becomes a symphony of nature. I just love to watch him digest. It's so simple, so direct. It's like the elements. Have you ever noticed how divinely he hitches his trousers up? Stomil admires authenticity too.

ALA: I know. It doesn't fascinate me very much. I'm afraid.

ELEANOR: You're too young. You haven't had time to learn the value of genuine simplicity. You will. It takes experience.

ALA: I'll certainly try. Tell me, Mother, do you think it's a good idea for me to marry Arthur?

ELEANOR: Oh, Arthur is something else again. He has principles.

ALA: But Stomil has principles too. You said so yourself. All that stuff about the right and duty to be happy.

ELEANOR: Oh, those were only opinions. Stomil has always detested principles. Arthur, on the other hand, has cast-iron principles.

ALA: And that's all he has.

ELEANOR: Ala, how can you say a thing like that? Arthur's the first man in fifty years to have principles. Doesn't that appeal to you? It's so original! And it's so becoming to him!

ALA: You really think principles are enough for me?

ELEANOR: Well, I admit, they're rather old-fashioned. But so unusual these days . . .

ALA: I'll take Arthur with principles if I have to, Mother. But principles without Arthur—no.

ELEANOR: But didn't he propose to you? Isn't he going to marry you?

ALA: Not Arthur.

ELEANOR: Then who? What are you talking about?

ALA: His principles!

ELEANOR: Then why did you accept?

ALA: Because I still have hope.

ELEANOR: That, my dear, is fatal.

EDDIE *enters with a stack of plates.*

EDDIE: May I continue?

ALA: Clatter away, Eddie boy. (*Corrects herself.*) I mean, yes, Edward, clàtter away. I mean, do continue, Edward.

ELEANOR: Tell me, Eddie, does it depress you? All these changes thought up by a bunch of fools?

EDDIE: Why should it depress me?

ELEANOR: Didn't I tell you? He's as free and natural as a butterfly. Oh, Eddie, you set the table so gracefully.

EDDIE: I'm not knocking myself out, that's for sure.

ALA: Eddie, come here.

EDDIE: At your service. What can I do for you, Miss?

Suddenly the bells fall silent.

ALA: Tell me, Eddie, have you got principles?

EDDIE: Principles? Sure.

ALA: What kind?

EDDIE: The best.

ALA: Tell me one. Please.

EDDIE: What's in it for me?

ALA: Well, can you or can't you?

EDDIE: If I have to, I guess. Just a sec. (*He puts the plates down on the floor and takes a little memo book from his pocket.*) I've got one written down here somewhere. (*He leafs through the book.*) Here it is! (*He reads.*) "I love you, and you're sound asleep."

ALA: That's all?

EDDIE: "You made your bed, now lie in it."

ALA: Oh, come on, Eddie. Read.

EDDIE: I did read. That's a principle.

ALA: Then read another!

EDDIE *giggles.*

What's so funny?

EDDIE: Well, there's one here . . .

ALA: Read it! . .

EDDIE: I can't, not in mixed company. It's too good.

ALA: And those are your principles?

EDDIE: Actually, no. I borrowed them from a friend who works for the movies.

ALA: You haven't got any of your own?

EDDIE (*proudly*): No.

ALA: Why not?

EDDIE: What do I need them for? I know my way around.

ELEANOR: Oh yes, Eddie. You certainly do.

> STOMIL *rushes in, pursued by* EUGENE *carrying a laced corset.* EDDIE *goes on setting the table.*

STOMIL: No, no! That's asking too much!

EUGENE: Take my word for it. You'll be glad once it's on.

ELEANOR: Now what's wrong?

STOMIL (*running from* EUGENE): He wants to strap me into that thing.

ELEANOR: What is it?

EUGENE: Great grandfather's corset. Indispensable. Pulls in the waist, guarantees a perfect figure for every occasion.

STOMIL: No, no, no. I'm wearing spats, I've got this collar on. What are you trying to do—kill me?

EUGENE: Now, Stomil, let's not do things by halves.

STOMIL: I've gone far enough. Let me live!

EUGENE: You're falling back into your old habits, Stomil. Come on. Stop making such a fuss. You admitted yourself you'd been putting on weight.

STOMIL: But I want to be fat! I want to live in harmony with nature!

EUGENE: You just don't want to be bothered. Come on. Don't fight it. It won't do any good.

STOMIL: Eleanor, save me!

ELEANOR: You don't think it might improve your looks?

STOMIL: My looks? What for? I'm a free fat artist.

> *He runs into his room.* EUGENE *following. The door closes behind them.*

ELEANOR: These perpetual scenes. And you say you still have hope?

ALA: Yes.

ELEANOR: And if you're only deluding yourself?

ALA: What difference does it make?

ELEANOR (*tries to take her in her arms*): My poor Ala! . . .

ALA (*freeing herself*): You don't need to pity me. I can take care of myself.

ELEANOR: But what if things don't work out?

ALA: That's my secret.

ELEANOR: You won't tell even me?

ALA: It will be a surprise.

STOMIL'S VOICE: Help!

ELEANOR: That's Stomil.

ALA: Uncle Eugene is really overdoing it. Do you think he has any influence on Arthur?

STOMIL'S VOICE: Let me go!

ELEANOR: I doubt it. It's probably the other way around.

ALA: Too bad. I thought it was all Uncle's fault.

STOMIL'S VOICE: Get out of here!

ELEANOR: I'd better go see what they're up to. I have a feeling something awful is going to happen.

ALA: So do I.

STOMIL'S VOICE: Murderer! Let me go!

ELEANOR: Good God, how will it all end?

STOMIL'S VOICE: No, no! I'll burst! I'll explode! Help!

ELEANOR: Eugene's going too far. But you, Ala, do be careful.

ALA: Careful?

ELEANOR: Don't go too far—like Uncle Eugene. (*She goes into Stomil's room.*)

ALA: Eddie, my veil!

EDDIE *hands her the veil and stands behind her. From Stomil's room screaming and the sound of a struggle are heard.* ARTHUR *enters.* ALA *and* EDDIE *don't notice him. Arthur's coat is open. He looks gray. His listless, unnatural movements show that he is having great difficulty keeping himself going. He carefully removes his coat and throws it down somewhere. Sits down in an armchair and sprawls out his legs.*

STOMIL'S VOICE: Damn you!

ARTHUR (*in a low, dull voice*): What's going on?

ALA *turns around.* EDDIE *dutifully picks up* ARTHUR'S *coat and goes out.*

ALA (*as though merely making an observation*): You're late.

ARTHUR *stands up and opens Stomil's door.*

ARTHUR: Let him go.

STOMIL, EUGENE *and then* ELEANOR *come out of the room.*

EUGENE: Why? It would have given him that final polish.

ARTHUR: I said let him go.

STOMIL: Thank you, Arthur. I'm glad to see you're not completely devoid of human feeling.

EUGENE: I protest!

ARTHUR *grabs him by the tie and pushes him back.*

ELEANOR: Arthur, what's happened? He's as pale as a ghost!

ARTHUR: You whited skeleton!

EUGENE: Arthur, it's me, it's your Uncle Eugene! Don't you know me? You and I together . . . the new life . . . saving the world. Don't you remember? You're choking me. You and I . . . together . . . Don't . .

ARTHUR (*pushing him back step by step*): You stuffed zero, you synthetic blob . . . you worm-eaten false bottom!

ELEANOR: Do something! He's choking him!

ARTHUR: You fake . . .

Mendelssohn's "Wedding March" resounds, loud and triumphant. ARTHUR *lets* EUGENE *go, picks up a carafe from the table and hurls it off stage where it lands with a loud crash. The march breaks off in the middle of a measure.* ARTHUR *sinks into an armchair.*

EDDIE (*enters*): Do you wish me to change the record?

ELEANOR: Who told you to put that on?

EDDIE: Mr. Eugene. His orders were to put it on as soon as Mr. Arthur entered the room.

EUGENE (*gasping for air*): My orders. Yes, that's right.

ELEANOR: We won't need any music right now.

EDDIE: As you wish, Madame. (*He goes out.*)

ARTHUR: It's a fraud . . . The whole thing . . . a fraud! (*He collapses.*)

STOMIL (*leans over him*): He's dead drunk.

EUGENE: That's a slander, an infamous slander. This young man knows his duty. He's the soul of moderation.

ELEANOR: I can't believe it either. Arthur never drinks.

STOMIL: Take it from me. I'm an expert.

ELEANOR: But why today of all days?

STOMIL: His last hours as a free man.

ALA *pours water into a glass and feeds it to* ARTHUR.

EUGENE: There must be some misunderstanding. It would be unwise to draw premature conclusions. The truth will soon be known.

STOMIL: Yes. If we wait just a minute, he'll explain. He was just getting started.

ELEANOR: Shh . . . he's coming to.

ARTHUR (*raises his head and points to* STOMIL): What on earth is that?

ELEANOR: He doesn't know his own father. Ohhh! (*She bursts into tears.*)

ARTHUR: Quiet, you females! It's not my parents I'm asking about. What's the meaning of this masquerade?

STOMIL. (*looking at his legs*): These . . . these are spats.

ARTHUR: Oh . . . yes, of course. They're spats. (*He sinks into thought.*)

EUGENE: Arthur's a little tired. Conditions will return to normal in a moment. Take your places. Attention! There will be no change in the program. (*To* ARTHUR *in a very friendly tone:*) Ha ha, well, Arthur, my boy, you were just joking, weren't you? Putting us to the test, you little devil! Don't worry. We won't abandon our positions. Here we are, all buttoned up from top to toe, once and for all. Stomil was even going to put on a corset. Cheer up, my boy. A little rest, and then . . . on with the wedding!

STOMIL: Same old song and dance! Can't you see, you ghost of the past, that he's stewed to the gills? His father's son all right.

EUGENE: That's a lie! Quiet! Come on, Arthur. It's time for action now. Everything's ready. Just one last step.

ARTHUR (*goes down on his knees to* STOMIL): Father, forgive me.

STOMIL: What's this? Some new trick?

ARTHUR (*dragging himself after* STOMIL *on his knees*): I was insane! There's no going back, no present, no future. There's nothing.

STOMIL (*evading him*): What is he now? A nihilist?

ALA (*tearing off her veil*): What about me? Am I nothing?

ARTHUR (*changing direction and dragging himself after her*): You too . . . forgive me!

ALA: You're a coward, that's all you are. A child and a coward and impotent!

ARTHUR: No, please don't say that. I'm not afraid, but I can't believe anymore. I'll do anything. I'll lay down my life . . . but there's no turning back to the old forms. They can't create a reality for us. I was wrong.

ALA: What are you talking about?

ARTHUR: About creating a world.

ALA: And me? Isn't anybody going to say anything about me?

EUGENE: This is treason!

ARTHUR (*changing direction again and heading for* EUGENE): You must forgive me too. I raised your hopes and I've let you down. But believe me, it's impossible . . .

EUGENE: I refuse to listen to this kind of talk. Pull yourself together. Stand up and get married. Raise a family, brush your teeth, eat with a knife and fork, make the world sit up straight. You'll see, we'll do it yet. You're not going to throw away our last chance, are you, Arthur?

ARTHUR: There never was a chance. We were wrong. It's hopeless.

EUGENE: Stomil's right. You're drunk. You don't know what you're saying.

ARTHUR: Yes, drunk. When I was sober I let myself be deceived, so I got drunk to dispel my illusions. You'd better have a drink too, Uncle

EUGENE: Me? Certainly not. . . . Well, perhaps just a little one. (*He pours himself a shot of vodka and downs it at one gulp.*)

ARTHUR: I had cold sober reasons for getting drunk. I drank myself sane again.

STOMIL: Nonsense. You got drunk out of despair.

ARTHUR: Yes, despair too. Despair that form can never save the world.

EUGENE: Then what can?

ARTHUR (*stands up, solemnly*): An idea!

EUGENE: What idea?

ARTHUR: If I only knew. Conventions always spring from an idea. Father was right. I'm a contemptible formalist.

STOMIL: Don't take it so hard, son. You know I've always been indulgent. Frankly, though, I've suffered plenty from your ideas. Thank God, that's all over now. (*Starts taking off his morning coat.*) Where are my pajamas?

ARTHUR (*rushes over to him and prevents him from taking off his coat*): Stop! A reversion to pajamas is equally impossible.

STOMIL: Why? Are you still trying to save us? I thought you'd got over that.

ARTHUR (*aggressively, going from one extreme to the other as drunks do; triumphantly*): Did you think I was going to cave in completely just like that?

STOMIL: Just a minute ago you were acting like a human being. Don't tell me you want to be an apostle again.

ARTHUR (*releasing* STOMIL, *with emphasis*): My sin was reason ... and abstraction, the lewd daughter of reason. Now I have drowned my reason in alcohol. I didn't get drunk the usual way. Though my aim was mystical, I drank most rationally. The fire water cleansed me. You've got to forgive me because I stand before you purified. I clothed you in vestments and tore them off again because they proved to be shrouds. But I will not abandon you, naked, to the gales of history; I'd rather have you curse me. Eddie!

EDDIE *enters.*

Shut the door.

ELEANOR: Yes, Eddie, shut the door, there's a draft.

ARTHUR: Don't let anybody leave.

EDDIE: Okay, boss.

STOMIL: This is a violation of civil rights!

ARTHUR: You want freedom? There is no freedom from life, and life is synthesis. You'd analyze yourselves to death. Luckily, however, you have me.

EUGENE: Arthur, you know I don't agree with Stomil. But aren't you going a little too far? I feel it's my duty to warn you. In spite of everything, I stand by the freedom of the individual.

ARTHUR: Good. Now what we need is to find an idea.

STOMIL (*simultaneously with* EUGENE *and* ELEANOR): Is this any way to treat your father?

EUGENE: I wash my hands of the whole business.

ELEANOR: Arthur, lie down for a while. I'll make you a nice cold compress.

ARTHUR: Until we come up with an idea, nobody leaves this room. Eddie. Guard the door!

EDDIE: Yes, sir.

Pause.

ELEANOR: Find him an idea, somebody, so he'll leave us alone. If I don't go to the kitchen, the cake will be burned to a crisp.

EUGENE: Better humor him.

ARTHUR: What do you suggest, Uncle?

EUGENE: Search me . . . God, maybe?

ARTHUR: That's been done. Lost His appeal.

EUGENE: True. Even in my time there wasn't much you could do with God. I grew up in an age of enlightenment and exact science. I only mentioned Him for the sake of form.

ARTHUR: Forget about form. What we're after now is a living idea.

EUGENE: How about sports? I used to ride horseback.

ARTHUR: Everybody goes in for sports nowadays. A lot of good it does them.

EUGENE: Sorry. Maybe Stomil has an idea.

STOMIL: Experiment. There's an idea.

ARTHUR: Please, this is serious.

STOMIL: Well, I'm serious too. Blazing trails, opening new frontiers! Man is always looking for new worlds to conquer and conquest comes from experiment. From trial and error. But always with an aim in view: the new life, radically new!

ARTHUR: A new life! I don't even know what to do with the old one.

STOMIL: Well, everything is still in the experimental stage, that's why.

EUGENE: Eleanor, have you got an idea?

ARTHUR: There's no sense asking a woman.

ELEANOR: I had an idea, but I've forgotten. I'm supposed to

look after everything. Why don't you ask Eddie? He's got a good head on his shoulders, and when he does say something, you can depend on it.

STOMIL: That's right. Eddie is the collective mind.

ARTHUR: Well, what do you say then, Eddie?

EDDIE: Well, if anybody were to ask me, I'd say progress, sir.

ARTHUR: Meaning what?

EDDIE: Well, just that, sir: progress.

ARTHUR: But what kind of progress?

EDDIE: The progressive kind, the kind that goes right ahead.

ARTHUR: You mean forward?

EDDIE: Right. With the front moving forward.

ARTHUR: And the back?

EDDIE: The back moving forward too. Right out there in front.

ARTHUR: Then the front is in back?

EDDIE: Depends on how you look at it. If you look from back to front, the front is in front, though somehow or other it's also in back.

ARTHUR: That doesn't sound very clear to me.

EDDIE: No. But it's progressive.

EUGENIA *enters, leaning on a cane.*

EUGENIA (*timidly*): There's something I must tell you . . .

ELEANOR: Not now, Mother. Can't you see the men are discussing politics?

EUGENIA: Just two words . . .

ARTHUR: No, I don't like it. I need an idea that naturally, inevitably, leads to form. Your kind of progress leads nowhere.

EUGENIA: Please listen to me, my darlings. I won't take much of your time.

STOMIL: What is it now?

ELEANOR: I don't know. Something's wrong with Mama.

STOMIL: Later. We're busy now. (*To* ARTHUR.) I still say we should get back to experiments. Then the idea will come by itself.

EUGENIA takes the knicknacks and napkins off the catafalque.

ELEANOR: What are you doing, Mama?

EUGENIA (*matter-of-factly*): I'm dying.

ELEANOR: Mother! That's not very funny, you know.

Silently EUGENIA tidies up the catafalque. She wipes away the dust with her sleeve.

Mother says she's dying.

EUGENE: What? Dying? Can't she see we're busy?

ELEANOR: Did you hear that, Mama?

EUGENIA: Help me.

Involuntarily ELEANOR gives her her arm. EUGENIA climbs up on the catafalque.

ELEANOR: But don't be silly, Mama. There's going to be a wedding today. You wouldn't want to spoil everything by dying, would you?

STOMIL: Dying? What's all this about death? I never thought about that . . .

ARTHUR (*to himself*): Death? Excellent idea! . . .

EUGENE: This is ridiculous, Eugenia. Pull yourself together. This is no way to behave.

ALA: It wouldn't be normal, Grandmother.

EUGENIA: I don't understand you people. You're all so intelligent, but if somebody wants to do something as simple as dying, you don't know what to make of it. Really, you are very strange people. (*She lies down on her back and folds her hands over her breast.*)

ELEANOR: Look at her. Do something . . . Maybe she's really . . .

EUGENE: Eugenia, this is carrying eccentricity too far. This sort of thing isn't done in our family.

STOMIL: It's sheer hypocrisy.

EUGENIA: You'll find the key to my room on the table. I won't need it anymore. I'll be able to come and go as I please. The cards are in the drawer. All marked . . .

ARTHUR: Death . . . the supreme form!

STOMIL: Not exactly viable, though, is it?

ARTHUR: Why not? When it's somebody else's death.

He seems to have had a revelation, beats his forehead.

Grandma, you're brilliant!

ELEANOR: You ought to be ashamed of yourself! You all ought to be ashamed of yourselves.

EUGENE: Eugenia, lie properly at least. You're all hunched up. Elbows at your sides. Or get up this minute. Dying is no way to behave in society. Death is irrational.

STOMIL: Death is final and therefore no good as an experiment. An experiment has to be repeatable. Of course, if you're only rehearsing, that's something else again. But even so, there's not much point in it.

ALA: Stop! Can't you see what's happening?

EUGENIA: Come closer, my children.

All except EDDIE *go over to the catafalque.*

Eddie, you too!

EDDIE *joins the others.*

Who are you?

EUGENE: We're . . . it's just us.

EUGENIA *starts giggling, first softly, then loudly.*

Now she's insulting us. Did I say something funny?

STOMIL: I'm not feeling so well myself. Must be a headache. (*He steps aside, feels his pulse, takes a mirror out of his pocket, and looks at his tongue.*)

ARTHUR: Thank you, Grandmother, I'll make use of your idea.

STOMIL (*putting the mirror away*): Nothing serious, I guess. Must be these tight clothes.

EUGENIA *dies.*

ELEANOR: Try again, Mama.

ARTHUR: She's dead. Strange. She was always so frivolous.

ALA: I can't stand it!

EUGENE: I don't understand.

STOMIL: I don't want to have anything to do with this.

ELEANOR: I never dreamed . . . Stomil, why didn't you warn me?

STOMIL: Of course, it's all my fault. Frankly I don't see that this changes anything at all. My collar's as tight as ever.

ARTHUR (*drawing the curtain in front of the catafalque*): Eddie, come here.

EDDIE *comes over and stands at attention.* ARTHUR *feels his muscle.*

You pack a good punch, don't you?

EDDIE: Not bad, sir.

ARTHUR: And if necessary, you could . . ? (*He runs his finger across his throat.*)

EDDIE (*phlegmatically after a pause*): You ask me a question, Mr. Arthur? I'm not sure I heard you right.

Pause. ARTHUR *laughs, unsure of himself, as though waiting to see.* EDDIE *laughs with a similar "ha ha."*

ARTHUR *laughs once again more loudly and with more assurance. Whereupon* EDDIE *utters a resounding laugh.* ARTHUR *slaps him on the shoulder.*

ARTHUR: Eddie, I like you. I've always liked you.

EDDIE: And I've always thought we'd understand each other someday.

ARTHUR: Then you do understand?

EDDIE: Eddie understands all right.

STOMIL: This business has rather upset me. I'm going to lie down for a while.

ARTHUR: Stay right where you are, Father.

STOMIL: Oh stop ordering me around, you little punk. I'm tired. (*He starts for his room.*)

ARTHUR: Eddie!

EDDIE *bars Stomil's way.*

STOMIL: Who do you think you are? (*Furiously pointing at* EDDIE, *to* ELEANOR:) And you've been having an affair with this flunky?

ELEANOR: For God's sake, not now. Not with Mama lying there.

EDDIE *pushes* STOMIL *into an armchair.*

ARTHUR: Just a bit more patience, please. It's all quite clear to me now. I shall show you the way to a better future.

EUGENE (*sitting down with resignation*): I just don't seem to care anymore . . . I must be getting old. We're just not as young as we used to be, are we, Stomil?

STOMIL: Speak for yourself. You're almost as old as Eugenia was, you old hypocrite. I feel fine. By and large. (*Pleading.*) Eleanor, where are you?

ELEANOR: Here, Stomil, right beside you.

STOMIL: Come here.

ELEANOR (*resting her hand on his forehead*): How do you feel?

STOMIL: I don't know what's wrong, but not well at all.

ARTHUR: Uncertainty and indecision are behind us now. Now the road lies before us, straight and clear. From now on there will be only one law and one herd.

STOMIL: What's he jabbering about now? . . . Oh, my head!

EUGENE: Something about a new legal code for livestock.

ARTHUR: Don't you see the logical conclusion? Ah, creatures of flesh, caught up in your glandular secretions and terrified at the thought of your death, *are you incapable of all understanding?* But I understand! Unthinking cattle, behold your redeemer! I have risen above this world, and I will draw you all up after me, because I alone have a brain freed from the snares of the bowels.

EUGENE: Instead of insulting us, my dear great-nephew, kindly express yourself more clearly.

ARTHUR: Won't you ever understand, you whose lives rot away like mushrooms? You're like blind puppies that would walk in circles forever if they had no master to lead them. Without form or ideas, you would crumble to chaos and be consumed by the void if I weren't on hand to save you. Do you know what I'm going to do with you? I'm going to create a system in which rebellion will be combined with order, nonbeing with being. I will transcend all contradictions.

EUGENE: It would perhaps be better if you'd just leave the room. You've disappointed me. It's all over between us. (*To himself.*) I'll probably return to writing my memoirs.

ARTHUR: Let me just ask you this: if nothing exists and if even rebellion is impossible, then what *can* be raised up out of this nothingness and made to exist?

EUGENE (*takes out a watch with a little chain*): It's late. We could all do with a bite to eat.

ARTHUR: Isn't anybody going to answer me?

STOMIL: Eleanor, what are we having for lunch today? I'd like something light. My stomach's a bit queasy. It's high time we took better care of it.

ELEANOR: You're right, Stomil. From now on we'll look after you. A little nap after lunch, a little stroll after napping. The morning will be for experiments.

STOMIL: And everything cooked in butter, or maybe cut out fats entirely.

ELEANOR: Yes. We'll sleep better that way too.

ARTHUR: What? Silence? All right, I'll tell you. (*He puts his chair on the set table, climbs reeling on the table and sits down in the chair.*)

ELEANOR: Careful of the dishes, Arthur.

ARTHUR: The only possible answer is power.

EUGENE: Power? What power? We're your family, remember?

STOMIL: He's raving. Don't pay any attention to him.

ARTHUR: Power alone can exist in a vacuum. Now I am up here above you, and you are beneath me.

EUGENE: Brilliant, isn't he?

ELEANOR: Arthur, come down. You're getting the table-cloth all dirty.

ARTHUR: You grovel beneath me in dust and ashes.

EUGENE: How long are we going to put up with this?

STOMIL: Let him talk. We'll take care of him after lunch. It's beyond me where he gets these tendencies. Must be his upbringing.

ARTHUR: Everything depends on being strong and decisive. I am strong. Look at me then. I am the answer to your dreams. Uncle Eugene, there will be order. Father, you have always rebelled, but your rebellion consumed itself in chaos. Now look at me. Power, too, is rebellion. A revolution in form and order, the revolt of the top against the bottom, the high against the low. The mountain needs the plain and the plain needs the mountain, otherwise each would cease to be what it is. Power resolves the paradox of opposites. Neither synthesis nor analysis, I am the act, the will and the way. I am power. I am above, within and beside all things. Give thanks to me for fulfilling the dreams of your youth. This is my gift to you. Yet I have a gift for myself as well: the form I have always longed for. For I can now create and destroy not just one but a thousand possible forms. I can incarnate and disincarnate myself. I have here within me—everything. (*He beats his breast.*)

EUGENE: Poor boy. Sad to see a thing like this happen.

STOMIL: Oh don't take it so seriously. Adolescent foolishness. Words, words, words. What power has he got over us?

EUGENE: Right! What does all his talk amount to anyway? We're united by blood, not by abstractions. He can't do a thing to us.

ARTHUR: It's very simple. I can kill you.

STOMIL (*rises from his chair and falls back again*): I absolutely forbid you . . . There are limits.

ARTHUR: Limits can be transcended. *You* taught me that. Power over life and death. What greater power can there be? A simple but profoundly important discovery!

EUGENE: Nonsense! I'll live as long as I please. That is, I mean, as long as it pleases. . . . I don't know whom, do you, Stomil?

STOMIL: Well . . . Nature?

EUGENE: Exactly. Nature or fate.

ARTHUR: No. *Me!*

EUGENE (*jumping up*): Don't make me laugh!

ARTHUR: But suppose I become your fate, Uncle?

EUGENE: Eleanor, Stomil, what does this mean? I won't stand for it. He's your son, after all.

ELEANOR: Look what you've done, Arthur. You've frightened your uncle. He's white as a sheet. Don't get up, Stomil. I'll get you a pillow.

ARTHUR: Did you really think I'd start something I couldn't finish? Each one of you has a death shut inside you like a nightingale locked in a cage. All I have to do is let it out. Well, do you still think I'm a utopian, a babbler, a dreamer?

EUGENE: Ha ha! There's no getting around it, Arthur— you've got a head on your shoulders. You've thought this whole thing out very nicely. Nothing like a good university education, I always say. Hopeless to argue with you; you'll always win. But while we talk, time is flying and though there's nothing I enjoy more than a philosophico-scientific discussion, especially with the younger generation, we've talked long enough. Our horizons have been expanded, but now it's time for something concrete. Enough theory. Let's have something to eat. What do you say, Eleanor?

ELEANOR: I wanted to suggest that some time ago, but I couldn't get a word in edgewise. Enough now, Arthur, come down. Or at least take your shoes off.

ARTHUR: You're right, Uncle, it's time for something concrete. Eddie, my dark angel, are you ready?

EDDIE: Ready, chief.

ARTHUR: Then grab him.

EUGENE (*trying to escape*): What are you going to do?

ARTHUR: First we're going to rub out Uncle Eugene.

ELEANOR: Rub out? Where on earth did you pick that up?

STOMIL: And now of all times, with my blood pressure sky-rocketing!

EUGENE (*still trying to reach the door*): Why me?

> EDDIE *bars the way.*

ARTHUR: So I'm all just theory, am I? Eddie, show him he's mistaken. You trash! What do you take me for?

> EDDIE *tries to catch* EUGENE.

EUGENE: This isn't a system. It's mob rule.

ARTHUR: Do your duty, Eddie.

EUGENE (*running from* EDDIE, *who follows him with sure, catlike movements*): What does this ape want of me? Keep your hands off me!

ARTHUR: He's not an ape. He's the right arm of my spirit, my word made flesh.

STOMIL (*tearing his collar open*): Eleanor, I feel awful. Eleanor!

ELEANOR: Look, your father's fainted.

EUGENE (*still running away*): Madman! Murderer!

ARTHUR (*stands up and stretches out his arm*): No! A man who has seen the one possibility and doesn't shrink from it. I am as pure as nature. I am free. Free!

ALA: Arthur! . . .

ARTHUR: Wait. First we've got to save the world.

ALA: I've been unfaithful to you. With Eddie.

> EDDIE *and* EUGENE *suddenly stop still and look at* ARTHUR *and* ALA. ELEANOR *is busy slapping Stomil's checks, trying to rouse him from his faint.*

ARTHUR (*slowly lowering his arms, after a moment of silence*): What?

ALA: I didn't think you'd mind. After all, you only wanted to marry me out of principle.

ARTHUR (*sits down, dazed*): When?

ALA: This morning.

ARTHUR (*to himself*): I see . . .

ALA: I didn't think you'd care. I thought . . . Look, I'm ready for the wedding. (*She puts on her veil.*) How do I look?

ARTHUR (*gropes his way clumsily off the table*): Wait a second, wait . . . You? You did that to me?

ALA (*with affected nonchalance*): I forgot to tell you. You were so busy . . . We can go now. Should I wear my gloves? They're a bit tight. You like the way I've done my hair?

ARTHUR (*bellowing*): You did that to *me*?

ALA (*affecting surprise*): You still going on about that? I didn't think you'd even be interested. Let's change the subject, shall we?

ARTHUR (*in a state of collapse, gropes his way around the table; he seems to have lost control over his movements; in a plaintive monotone*): How could you . . . how could you?

ALA: But you said you only needed me to help you with your plan. Don't you remember? I didn't misunderstand you, did I? Yesterday, when we were talking and you said such clever things, I was impressed. Really. Eddie could never have spoken like that.

ARTHUR (*bellowing*): Eddie!

ALA: Eddie's something else again.

ARTHUR (*plaintively*): Why did you do that to me?

ALA: What's got into you, darling? I've told you, I didn't think you'd care. Frankly, I'm surprised at you, making such a fuss over nothing. Now I'm sorry I even told you.

ARTHUR: But why?

ALA: Oh, my stubborn darling! I had my reasons.

ARTHUR (*shouting*): What reasons?

ALA: Let's forget about it. You're just getting yourself all worked up.

ARTHUR: Tell me!

ALA: I only wanted to . . .

ARTHUR: Go on. Your reasons . . .

ALA (*frightened*): Oh, the stupidest, silliest little reasons . . .

ARTHUR: Go on!

ALA: I won't tell you. You always get mad.

ARTHUR: Oh God!

ALA: If you want, we'll never say another word about the whole thing. Is it all my fault?

ARTHUR (*goes up to* STOMIL *and* ELEANOR): Why are you all against me? What have I done to you? Mother, did you hear that?

ELEANOR: Ala, I warned you.

ARTHUR (*clinging to* ELEANOR): Mama, tell her she mustn't do such things. Do something, help me, I can't live like this. Tell her . . . How can she treat me like this . . . (*He bursts into tears.*)

ELEANOR (*tearing herself away from him*): Get away from me, you silly child.

ARTHUR (*repulsed, staggers to the center of the stage; tearfully*): I wanted to save you. I was so close . . . And now you've ruined it all. Ah, the world is evil, evil, evil.

ALA: Come to me, Arthur! (*She goes toward him.*) Oh, my poor boy, I feel so sorry for you.

ARTHUR (*shoving her away*): You! Sorry for me? You dare to pity me? I don't need anyone's pity. You don't know me yet . . . but you're going to now. All right.

You've rejected my idea. You've trampled me under-
foot. (*To* ALA.) And you besmirched the noblest idea
in all history, you goose! Oh! What blindness! You
can't even begin to imagine who it is you've lost. And
who did you do it with? With this half-witted punk,
this garbage dumped out by our times. I'll go away,
but I won't leave you behind in this world. You don't
know what you're living for anyway. Where is he, your
darling lover? Where's that rotten beer belly anyway?
I'll fix that early bird's guts! (*He runs desperately
around the room, looking blindly for something on the
tables and on the sofa.*) The revolver! Where can it
be? It's impossible to find anything with all this
damned order! Mama, have you seen the revolver?

EDDIE *creeps up from behind, takes the revolver from
his breast pocket, and, taking a wide swing, hits
ARTHUR in the back of the neck with the butt. ARTHUR
sinks to his knees. EDDIE tosses the revolver aside,
pushes Arthur's head deftly forward so that it hangs
down, clasps his hands and, raising himself on his
tiptoes, swings his hands down on Arthur's head like
an ax. ARTHUR falls over, hitting the floor with his forehead. This scene must look very realistic.*

ALA (*kneels beside* ARTHUR): Arthur!
ELEANOR (*kneels on the other side of* ARTHUR): Arthur! My
son!
EDDIE (*steps aside, looks at his hands, with surprise*): Hm,
that was hard.
ARTHUR (*slowly and softly, as though amazed*): Strange . . .
everything's disappeared . . .
ALA: But I didn't want . . . It's not true!
EDDIE: Ha ha ha!

ARTHUR (*still with his face on the floor, very softly*): I loved you, Ala.

ALA: Why didn't you tell me before?

EDDIE: "I love you and you're sound asleep."

ELEANOR (*runs to* STOMIL *and shakes him*): Wake up. Your son is dying!

STOMIL (*opening his eyes*): Can't you people spare me anything?

He stands up with difficulty and leaning on ELEANOR *approaches* ARTHUR. ELEANOR, STOMIL *and* EUGENE *stand over him.* ALA *kneels.* EDDIE *to one side makes himself comfortable in an armchair.*

ARTHUR (*stretching out on the floor*): I wanted . . . I wanted . . . (*pause*).

ALA (*stands up; matter-of-factly*): He's dead.

EUGENE: Perhaps he's better off. He nearly murdered his uncle.

STOMIL: Forgive him. He wasn't happy.

EUGENE (*magnanimously*): Oh, I don't bear him any grudge. He can't hurt me now.

STOMIL: He tried to overcome indifference and mediocrity. He lived for reason, but lived too passionately. He died because his thought had betrayed his feelings.

EDDIE: He meant well, but he was too highstrung. His kind never gets old.

All turn toward EDDIE.

STOMIL: Hold your tongue, you scoundrel, and get out of my house. You ought to be glad to get off so easy.

EDDIE: Why should I leave? I'll say it again: he meant well. I'm staying.

STOMIL: Why?

EDDIE: It's my turn now. Now you're all going to listen to me.

STOMIL: We listen? To you?

EDDIE: Sure, why not? You've seen that I pack a wicked punch. Nothing to worry about so long as you keep quiet and do what I say. You'll see. You won't have to worry. I'm a regular guy. I like a joke, like a good time. But get this: There's got to be order.

EUGENE: We're in for it now.

EDDIE: You know, you talk too much. Take my shoes off for me, will you?

EUGENE: I submit to brute force. But I'll despise him in my heart.

EDDIE: Go ahead and despise me, but now take my shoes off, and quick.

EUGENE *kneels in front of him and takes his shoes off.*

STOMIL: I've always thought we were slaves of abstractions, but that someday humanity would take its revenge. Now I see that it's only Eddie.

ELEANOR: Maybe it won't be so bad. He certainly won't mind if you diet.

EUGENE (*holding the shoes*): Should I shine them, sir?

EDDIE: No, you can have 'em. I'm changing anyway. (*He stands up, takes off Arthur's jacket, puts it on and looks at himself in the mirror.*) A little tight, but not bad!

STOMIL: Come, Eleanor. We're only a poor old couple now.

EDDIE: Don't go too far, and be ready to come running when I call.

ELEANOR: Are you coming with us, Ala?

ALA: I'm coming. He loved me, nobody can take that away from me.

STOMIL (*to himself*): We may as well assume it was love.
ALA: Did you say something, Father ?
STOMIL: Me? No.

> ELEANOR *and* STOMIL *go out, holding hands.* ALA *follows.* EDDIE *takes various poses and expressions before the mirror, thrusts out his lower jaw, puts one hand on his hip.* EUGENE *runs up and down with Eddie's shoes, finally stops beside* ARTHUR.

EUGENE: I've got the feeling, Arthur, my boy, that nobody needs you anymore.

> *He stands there meditating.* EDDIE *goes out and comes back with a tape recorder. Puts it on the table and plugs it in. Immediately the tango "La Cumparsita" resounds very loud and clear. It must be this tango and no other.*

EDDIE: Well, Uncle Eugene, would you like to dance?
EUGENE: Me? With you . . . Oh, all right, why not?

> EUGENE *puts down the shoes beside* ARTHUR. EDDIE *puts his arm around him. They take the proper position, wait out one measure and start dancing.* EDDIE *leads. They dance.* EUGENE *still has the red carnation in his buttonhole.* EDDIE *in Arthur's jacket that is too tight for him, his powerful arms protruding from the sleeves that are too short. He has taken* EUGENE *by the waist. They dance all the figures of the tango. The curtain falls. "La Cumparsita" is still heard. As the light goes on in the theater, the tune issues from numerous loudspeakers throughout the house.*

VATZLAV

A Play in 77 Scenes

Translated by Ralph Manheim

Cast of Characters

VATZLAV

MR. BAT

MRS. BAT

BOBBIE

THE LACKEY

QUAIL

SASSAFRAS

THE GENIUS

THE GUIDE

JUSTINE

THE OFFICER

GENERAL BARBARO

OEDIPUS

THE EXECUTIONER

SOLDIERS

VOICES

Vatzlav received its world premiere production at the Theater am Neumarkt in Zurich on February 11, 1970. It was directed by Felix Rellstab. The role of Mrs. Bat was played by a man, Michael Rittermann. Other principals in the first performance cast were Werner Dahms (Vatzlav), Hans Wyprächter (Sassafras), Paul Bühlmann (Quail), and Christina Amun (Justine). The play has also been mounted by the Nederlandse Comedie in Amsterdam, at the Thalia Theater in Hamburg, in Berlin, Göttingen, Cologne, and other European cities.

The first North American performance was given in August 1970 at the Stratford Festival, Stratford, Ontario, Canada. All of the performers wore half-masks and the role of Mrs. Bat was played by a woman. The principal performers were Douglas Campbell (Vatzlav), Richard Curnock (General Barbaro), James Edmond (The Genius), Donald Ewer (Sassafras), Roland Hewgill (Oedipus), Eric House (Quail), William Needles (Bobbie), Kate Reid (Mrs. Bat), Arnold Soboloff (Mr. Bat), and Carolyn Younger (Justine). Colin George was the director, Brian Jackson was the designer, and Lou Applebaum was the music director.

All photographs published inside the book are by Douglas Spillane of the Stratford Festival production.

The stage, consisting of a platform inclined toward the audience, is empty. The indications "right" and "left" are always from the audience's point of view.

SCENE 1

Half light. Thunder and lightning. VATZLAV *appears upstage and climbs up on the platform. He is a powerfully-built man in his forties with blond hair. He is wearing a white collarless shirt of coarse material and trousers with frayed edges reaching halfway between his knees and ankles. He is barefoot. He steps forward and speaks to the audience.*

VATZLAV: I was a slave and now I'm shipwrecked. An outcast slave and now a castaway. Condemned to slavery, set free by a shipwreck, finding, when all was lost, my freedom, yet too lost and battered to enjoy my freedom . . . Maybe a rest would help. (*He sits down on the ground.*) In the storm today, a slave ship foundered off the coast. I don't know what coast this is, but it must be far from my country. Taking advantage of the disaster, I swam ashore—well, to tell the truth, the sea threw me up on the sand. Everyone else drowned.

MAN'S VOICE (*off stage, right*): He-elp!

VATZLAV: Not all of them, apparently! Hey! You alive?

MAN'S VOICE: I'm drowning!

VATZLAV: Just what I said. He's drowning like the rest. Me, I'm saved. By decision of Providence. If there is a Providence. There must be, because if there's been a decision, it must come from somewhere. If it was a decision. Forget it. It's facts that count, and the fact is I didn't drown.

MAN'S VOICE: I'm drowning . . .

VATZLAV: Quit bragging. You should've seen me when I was drowning.

MAN'S VOICE: Help!

VATZLAV: I'd help him if there was a Providence that meant me to save the poor bastard. But it doesn't look like it. On the contrary. It looks as if Providence had made up its mind to let him drown, and who am I to meddle with its decision? Assuming, of course, that there is a Providence, and in this case I'll bet money there is.

MAN'S VOICE: Oh! . . . Oh! . . .

VATZLAV: That proves it. The man's in trouble.

MAN'S VOICE: Countryman!

VATZLAV: Countryman? Yes, he's from my country. I could save him if Providence weren't against it. Suppose I bucked Providence? Then what? I'd have a witness to my slavery. Wherever I went, his eyes would say to me: "I remember, old friend." Once freed, a single slave can forget. A second slave won't let him. Conclusion: Providence wants the second to drown so he can't interfere with the first.

MAN'S VOICE: Friend!

VATZLAV: Friend? If you're my friend, leave me alone. Does a friend stand in a friend's way? What kind of a friend is it that keeps reminding you that you were once a slave? You're no friend of mine and you're no friend of freedom if you insist on living and poisoning other people's freedom. If you were a real friend, you'd realize that I don't need you. (*He stands up.*) New life, I salute you!

MAN'S VOICE: Traitor!

VATZLAV: Traitor? Whom have I betrayed? Did I promise anyone not to escape if I could? No. My guards swore I'd never escape. If I've escaped, it's the guards who haven't kept their word. Or did I swear to my fellow slaves that I'd drown with them if the ship was wrecked? No. There was no such agreement between us. Whom could I betray? Only the Providence that has chosen me. That I will never do. I will go to meet my destiny, and I will say . . .

MAN'S VOICE: I'm dying!

VATZLAV: Here I am. Destiny, you want me to be free . . . But come to think of it, what for? What can you do with freedom? . . . I'd better think this over. (*He paces the stage.*) What do free men do? (*He counts on his fingers.*) They make money, they win honor and glory. They've done it since the beginning of the world. Slaves are the only ones who don't because they're forbidden to. I see. Providence is showing me the way. Providence wants me to be rich, powerful, and happy. And you think you can prevent me, you envious hunk of fish bait? (*He raises one arm towards heaven as though to grasp a hand that is extended to him.*) Okay, it's a deal. (*He raises three fingers and swears.*) Providence, I swear to you, you will not be disappointed. You can count on me. (*Thunder and lightning.*) There's the answer. That's our pact.

MAN'S VOICE: Save me!

VATZLAV: Try to see it my way, pal. I've sworn an oath. (*He listens. Silence.*) He's caught on. No more witness. No one to prevent me from starting a new life. Nobody knows me here. If anybody asks me who I am and where I came from, I'll introduce myself as a traveler of noble family. Isn't it my right? Suffering ennobles. After all they've put me through, I've got the makings of several princes with enough left over for a good-sized duke. In our country they say all foreigners are of noble family. It must be true, because in our country there's nothing but riffraff. Since foreigners aren't us, they must be rich and noble.

Vatzlav's double, a dummy rolling on the ground as if tossed by waves, appears upstage.

You still here? Get away! You belong in the ocean.

The double rolls up to Vatzlav's feet.

Is he stubborn! (*Kicks him.*) If he's dead, why doesn't he sink? Why doesn't he lie quietly on the bottom? What will people think if they see me in such company? A stiff! And a low-class stiff at that. (*He takes the dummy by the feet and draws him to the "shore."*) How can I prove he's no relation? . . . Somebody's coming . . . Say, get a look at that rig. He must be a duke.

SCENE 2

Enter left THE LACKEY *in violet livery and white stockings. He is carrying a tray with two glasses of champagne. Seeing* VATZLAV *and the drowned man, he stops.*

VATZLAV: Morning, Duke . . .

He bows very low; THE LACKEY *bows, too.* THE LACKEY *looks at the drowned man (the dummy).*

Look, your highness, look at the pretty sea gull.

VATZLAV *points to the sky and* THE LACKEY *raises his eyes.*

Why look at the ground when the sky is so beautiful?

THE LACKEY *looks down at the drowned man.*

Look, Duke, I'm a great dancer.

VATZLAV *performs a few leaps and dance steps.* THE LACKEY *watches him but soon turns his eyes toward the drowned man.*

Hm . . . He prefers the stiff. Is the stiff better than me? What's so interesting about him? . . . Look, Duke, if you must look at the ground, look—a shell. Here . . . (VATZLAV *picks up an imaginary shell.*) Isn't it lovely?

THE LACKEY *bows, as does* VATZLAV. THE LACKEY *exits left.*

SCENE 3

VATZLAV (*tosses the imaginary shell after* THE LACKEY, *then he bows ironically*): You call that a duke? He didn't rap me in the mouth. If he'd have kicked me at least, or insulted me. No, not a word. He's a fraud. I suppose they're all frauds in this country. They won't fool me again. I'll show 'em who's noble around here. (*To the drowned man.*) You again? Split! Bury yourself! Heave ho! (*He draws the dummy to the shore and throws it into the water.*)

SCENE 4

Enter left MR. *and* MRS. BAT, *both in their forties.* MR. BAT
wears black evening clothes, top hat, white gloves, and spats.
In one hand he holds a black cane with a white handle, in
the other a glass of champagne. He is smoking a cigar. MRS.
BAT *is ostentatiously beautiful. She wears a pink crinoline*
very low at the neck, a complicated hair-do, and lots of
jewelry. In one hand she carries an open parasol, in the
other a glass of champagne.

MR. BAT: Ho, my good man. Have you seen a corpse by any
  chance?
VATZLAV: A what?
MR. BAT: I hear a body has been washed up on the beach.
VATZLAV: Who?
MR. BAT (*to* MRS. BAT): He seems to be deaf.
MRS. BAT: Or drunk. Foreigners are often drunk.
MR. BAT (*to* VATZLAV): A corpse. I wish to see it.
VATZLAV: See it?
MR. BAT (*to* MRS. BAT): If he's not deaf, he's crazy.
MRS. BAT: Quite possibly. Foreigners are often crazy.
VATZLAV: See it? Down on your knees. Kiss the dust and do
  homage. That's what you can do.
MR. BAT: I'm losing my patience.
MRS. BAT: My dear sir, my husband's question was prompted
  by pure kindness. If his words have upset you, do con-
  trol your anger and answer politely. I, too, should like
  to know.

VATZLAV: He's fortunate in having a charming lady to intercede for him. I'd have strangled him. But now listen, both of you, pay close attention, or I won't bear the consequences.

He takes Mr. Bat's cigar and smokes it with obvious pleasure.

Our ship sank in the storm today. Do you know what a ship is?

MRS. BAT: We choose to ignore that question.

VATZLAV: You don't know. If you never saw our ship, you haven't any idea what a ship really is. Fifty masts. So many sails there was room for thirty winds at the same time, and no crowding. As for the guns, you couldn't even count them. Every day we tossed two or three of them overboard just for the hell of it, for the splash, and there were always plenty left. The prow was pure gold.

MRS. BAT: Gold?

VATZLAV (*takes Mr. Bat's glass of champagne, drinks, and then returns it*): It was a royal ship. It belonged to a king. Down on your knees! He was a big dictator.

MRS. BAT: How big?

VATZLAV: The biggest in the world. We sailed the seven seas and wherever nations saw our flag they bowed down to it.

MRS. BAT: Why did they do that?

VATZLAV: Because he liked it.

MRS. BAT: Where is he now?

VATZLAV (*pointing to the ground*): Here, in this tomb. Oh, poor Daddy!

MRS. BAT: Daddy?

VATZLAV: I am his son. O, cruel sea! An orphan's tears are

saltier than your waters and more abundant. I will drown you, O sea, in my ocean.

MRS. BAT (*to* MR. BAT): How bereaved he is!

VATZLAV: Thank you, ma'am.

MR. BAT (*to* MRS. BAT): He must be lying.

VATZLAV: Take care how you speak to the king's son!

MRS. BAT: But how did you escape?

VATZLAV: We fought the tempest, but in vain. The waves beat down upon the deck. I saw the ship was sinking. My first thought was for the king, my father. "Daddy, climb upon my back. I'll save you." Thus I leapt into the sea and like a dolphin I cut through the angry waves. (VATZLAV *makes swimming movements.*) For me to swim ashore was child's play. "Daddy," I said, "alight." But he lay still. I turned my head. No, no. I can't go on . . .

MRS. BAT: But he couldn't have drowned. What happened?

VATZLAV: Poisoned.

MRS. BAT: Poisoned in mid-ocean?

VATZLAV: I was rocking and pitching. He took some seasickness pills. Alas, he took too many. Don't make me go on . . . It's too painful.

MR. BAT: And the ship?

VATZLAV: It sank.

MR. BAT: Such a magnificent ship. It doesn't seem possible.

VATZLAV: There was a hole.

MR. BAT: In such a beautiful ship?

VATZLAV: The most beautiful hole ever seen.

MR. BAT (*to* MRS. BAT): What shall we do with him?

MRS. BAT: Give him a few coppers.

VATZLAV: What? Coppers for a king's son?

MR. BAT: You see, he refuses.

VATZLAV: Maybe if you said silver . . .

MRS. BAT: The poor man!

MR. BAT (*taking his wife's arm*): I've given him my cigar . . .

They move to the left.

VATZLAV: Hey! What about the bread?

MR. BAT: He can smoke it.

VATZLAV (*runs after them and bars the way*): I'm not asking for any presents.

He holds out the cigar to MR. BAT.

Here, I'll sell it to you.

MR. BAT: Thank you, but I have more.

VATZLAV: Couldn't you give me a job?

MR. BAT: I don't employ persons of good family.

VATZLAV: I'm practically nothing on my mother's side. She was a cook.

MRS. BAT: Haven't you some little job for him?

MR. BAT (*stopping*): What can you do?

VATZLAV: Everything.

MR. BAT: That's too much.

MR. *and* MRS. BAT *again begin to walk away.*

VATZLAV: No, no, not everything. I can do certain things.

MR. BAT (*stopping*): For instance . . .

VATZLAV: I can cheer. (*He claps his hands.*) Long live! Long live!

MR. BAT: Who?

VATZLAV: Anybody.

MR. BAT: What else?

VATZLAV: Or . . . (*He shouts.*) Down with! Down with! . . . I can do that, too.

MR. BAT: Down with whom?

VATZLAV: You're the boss.

MR. BAT: Not interested.

MR. *and* MRS. BAT *start off again.*

VATZLAV (*barring their way*): I can imitate animals. (*He crows like a rooster.*)

MR. BAT: You're out of tune.

VATZLAV *barks.*

That's better.

VATZLAV: I can roar, too.

MR. BAT (*stopping*): Roar? Let's hear you.

VATZLAV *roars.*

Hm, not bad.

VATZLAV: You mean, maybe . . .

MR. BAT: I'll see what I can do . . .

MRS. BAT *whispers in his ear.*

But will he make the grade?

VATZLAV: I'll make the grade. Don't you worry.

MR. BAT: Get down on all fours.

VATZLAV *complies.*

What do you think?

MRS. BAT: I think he's lovely.

MR. BAT: Trot!

VATZLAV *trots on all fours.*

Good. You're hired.

VATZLAV: Thanks, boss.

MR. BAT: From now on, you're a bear.

VATZLAV: I'd rather be a hound.

MR. BAT: I have a large pack, but there's nothing to hunt. I need game.

VATZLAV: You mean? . . . Exactly what will I have to do?

MR. BAT: Run around the woods like a bear . . .

VATZLAV: Nothing else?

MR. BAT: And roar from time to time . . .

VATZLAV: That's easy.

MR. BAT: To frighten the sheep.

VATZLAV: Leave it to me. They won't have a minute's peace. Is that all?

MR. BAT: That's all. (*He takes a coin from his pocket.*) Here's an advance.

VATZLAV (*examining the coin*): What? Only one? For such a difficult animal?

MR. BAT: You'll get the balance later.

VATZLAV (*pocketing the coin*): Okay, it's a deal . . . By the sweat of thy brow . . .

MR. BAT: But remember, no talking. You're an animal now and mum's the word. Forget that you understand what people say. Forget you have a tongue.

VATZLAV (*sticking out his tongue*) Ahhh . . .

MR. BAT: Put it away and shut up. (*To* MRS. BAT.) Now we have a bear.

They exit left.

SCENE 5

VATZLAV (*sticking his tongue out at them*): Ahhh . . . "Now we have a bear." Hear that, Daddy? Never thought I'd sink so low, did you? But it might have been worse. (*Boastfully.*) I'm lord of the forest . . . all the other animals are my vassals. Now I'll visit my kingdom. Forest, watch your step, here comes your master. (*He exits left.*)

SCENE 6

Enter right BOBBIE, *a sturdy man in his forties. He wears a little boy's sailor suit—much too tight for him—blue blouse with a wide collar, short blue trousers, white knee socks, and black shoes. He is holding a hoop and a stick. He has a ring on one finger and around his neck hangs a gold watch suspended on a chain.*

BOBBIE: Oh, when will Daddy and Mummy get back? I don't like it when they go off by themselves. I dreamt about Daddy last night. He was holding a fork in one hand and a knife in the other. Then Mummy came in with a frying pan. Daddy sharpened the knife on the fork and Mummy rubbed me with butter. They put me in the frying pan. "Daddy," I asked, "is it a surprise?" And Daddy said: "It needs marjoram." "Daddy," I asked, "why marjoram?" "You're too young, you'll understand later on." And before I could say "Jack Robinson" I was seasoned. With marjoram and other spices. "Look," said Mummy, "he's getting all red." "Splendid," said Daddy, "he tastes best when he's red."

SCENE 7

Enter right MR. *and* MRS. BAT.

BOBBIE: Oh, Mummy, Mummy!

He hugs MRS. BAT.

MR. BAT: Why are you so red?

MRS. BAT (*placing her hand on Bobbie's forehead*): Your little face is on fire.

MR. BAT (*aside*): Red, in my house?

MRS. BAT: How pink you are . . .

BOBBIE: Pink?

MRS. BAT: As a red rose.

MR. BAT (*aside*): Oh! A rose!

BOBBIE: It's because I'm so glad to see you both again. (*Aside.*) Oh, my goodness, I've told a lie.

MR. BAT: We're glad, too. (*Aside.*) Those ruddy cheeks arouse my desires. But heavens, he's my son. Oh, if only he were green.

MRS. BAT: That flesh-and-blood color is so becoming to you . . .

MR. BAT: Stop!

BOBBIE: It's becoming to you, too, Mummy.

MRS. BAT: Silly boy, I'm always so pale.

BOBBIE: But now you're blushing.

MRS. BAT: That's odd.

BOBBIE: If I'm like a rose, you're like a . . .

MR. BAT: Stop!

MRS. BAT: What's the matter?

BOBBIE: He's as white as a sheet.

MR. BAT: I'm thirsty.

BOBBIE: I'll get you some water.

MR. BAT: Water? Ha, ha!

BOBBIE: A glass of wine?

MR. BAT: Wine? Ha, ha!

BOBBIE: Or some sherbet?

MR. BAT: Sherbet? Ha, ha! I want . . . raspberries!

BOBBIE: I'll go get raspberries.

MR. BAT: Don't bother.

BOBBIE: I'll tell the butler to bring you a whole bowl of them.

MR. BAT: They've got to be fresh.

BOBBIE: I'll go to the woods.

MR. BAT: You stay here. We'll go.

BOBBIE: I'll go with you.

MR. BAT: No, we wish to be alone.

BOBBIE: Always by yourselves.

MR. BAT: Goodby.

MR. *and* MRS. BAT *exit left.*

MR. BAT'S VOICE (*off stage*): Raspberries! Raspberries!

SCENE 8

BOBBIE: Mummy and Daddy have a secret. They're hiding something. Who are they hiding it from? From me. Who am I? A child. So it must be a secret that's not for children. It must be a sin. What? Can it be that my parents are sinners? But it's sinful of me to think such thoughts. I'd better stop or I won't be a good boy any more. But if my parents are sinners, how can I be a good boy? On the other hand, I could be the wicked child of good parents. Or worse! I could be the good child of wicked parents. In the first case, I would be wronging them. In the second case, they would be wronging me. Either way, you'd have injustice. Only a good boy of good parents or a wicked boy of wicked parents can meet the requirements of justice.

MR. BAT'S VOICE (*off stage*): Raspberries! Raspberries!

BOBBIE: What are they up to in the woods? I'll follow them. (*He exits left.*)

SCENE 9

Enter right VATZLAV *wearing a bear mask.*

VATZLAV: Whew! . . . Why did I get mixed up in this bear business? You run yourself ragged. I wouldn't wish it on my worst enemy. A shoemaker or a tailor can sit by the fire and no one finds fault with his work. Suppose I sat by the fire. Oh no, a bear's got to roam the woods. Who ever saw a bear outside of the woods?

A VOICE (*off stage*): Me.

VATZLAV: Ho! Who dares to contradict me, the king of the forest?

SCENE 10

Enter left QUAIL, *the peasant.*

QUAIL: Your humble servant.

VATZLAV: Poor devil, come closer. Do you know whom you are addressing?

QUAIL: You bet. His lordship, the bear.

VATZLAV: Well spoken.

QUAIL: His worship, the bear.

VATZLAV: You seem to be an intelligent animal. Who are you?

QUAIL: Quail.

VATZLAV: A low-class bird. A quail can't hold a candle to a bear.

QUAIL: I'm not a bird. I'm a man.

VATZLAV: Are you sure?

QUAIL: Sure as shit.

VATZLAV: A quail-man?

QUAIL: Quail's my name. It runs in the family.

VATZLAV: That doesn't prove anything. What do you do for a living?

QUAIL: I work in the boss' fields.

VATZLAV: Hm. A peasant. Never mind. The royal bear deigns to talk to the humble peasant. See here, Quail, did you say you saw a bear outside the woods?

QUAIL: Well, not exactly. I've seen his skin, though.

VATZLAV: Is that a joke?

QUAIL: It's a funny thing about a bear and his skin. He's not always in it. Sometimes, you see, the skin's in one place and the bear's someplace else.

VATZLAV: Do they hunt much around here?

QUAIL: Yup. When there's game.

VATZLAV: Quail, dear Mr. Quail, take me with you.

QUAIL: God forbid. Your place is in the boss' woods. I'd be in a fine fix if the game warden found your skin in my hut. They're hard on poachers in these parts.

VATZLAV: That's not what I meant. I'll work for you, I'll milk your cows . . .

QUAIL: Oh, no.

VATZLAV: Mind the children, chop wood . . .

QUAIL: Can't be done. You belong to the boss.

VATZLAV: Tell me this, at least. Is he a hard master?

QUAIL: He's easier on bears than on people. (*He exits left.*)

SCENE 11

VATZLAV (*removes his bear mask*): So . . . it could be worse. But it's pretty bad all the same. When there's game, they hunt. Better to be a slave than to lose my skin in freedom. Maybe prison isn't so bad. You keep warm, they let you breathe, even if the stench turns your stomach. Did a man ever die of disgust? No. But plenty of men have died because they were disgusted with disgust. Served them right. That's the sin of pride, thinking you're better than other people. "Maybe this is okay for other people, but, personally, I can't stand it." That's what they say. God gave all men a nose to smell with, so why rebel against equality? Where do you find more equality than in prison? If we're all equal by nature, nature must want us to be in prison and not free. Morality, too, because you can starve in freedom but in prison they always fed me. I'm beginning to think I didn't really appreciate prison. A peaceful life, a secure old age—that's what I gave up. The hunters will come and kill me. What good is freedom when you're not the hunter but the hunted? Down with hunters! Long live bears!

SCENE 12

Enter right MR. *and* MRS. BAT.

MR. BAT: What's that again?

VATZLAV (*putting his mask on*): Long live hunters!

MR. BAT: Your orders were to be silent. Why are you shouting?

VATZLAV: Oh, master, I was thinking what a beautiful thing the hunt is. Ah, the hunt. The horns . . . the hounds . . .

MR. BAT: You're to keep quiet. Understand?

VATZLAV: But I can't. The sound of horns in the early morning, the joyous cries of the beaters—the thought of it filled me with such delight, such love for the hunters, even for the hounds, I couldn't help shouting . . .

MR. BAT: Enough!

VATZLAV: Long live the hunt!

MR. BAT: Silence!

VATZLAV: I will be silent, but the rapture of my heart cannot be stilled. No one can prevent me from loving in secret. Oh, hunters, how long must I await you?

MR. *and* MRS. BAT *exit left.*

SCENE 13

VATZLAV (*taking off the mask*): Maybe I overdid it. What if they unleash the pack? Here they come. No, it's a little boy.

SCENE 14

Enter right BOBBIE.

BOBBIE: So here I am in the forest. I can't see three steps ahead of me. But I won't turn back. I don't know what's in store for me here, at home I know everything. There's no hope when you know everything.

VATZLAV: He looks flabby and stupid.

BOBBIE: O forest, forest, you've given me hope.

VATZLAV: I'll bet he's a coward.

BOBBIE: A hope of hope.

VATZLAV: I'll scare him out of his wits. Good God! That's the only pleasure I have left.

He puts on the mask, bounds in front of BOBBIE *and roars.*

BOBBIE: Why are you roaring?

VATZLAV *roars louder.*

Are you in pain?

VATZLAV *roars louder still.*

Don't you feel well?

VATZLAV (*removing his mask*): You little snot, can't you see I'm a bear?

BOBBIE: Really? That's too bad. Then go ahead and roar.

VATZLAV: Aren't you afraid?

BOBBIE: Not at all.

VATZLAV: But I'm a wild beast. Why aren't you afraid?

BOBBIE: That's just it. I know who you are and when I know something, it doesn't frighten me.

VATZLAV: What if I ate you up?

BOBBIE: Then I'd be eaten. I'd be even less frightened than now.

VATZLAV: You lack experience. I remember when even the dead were afraid because they didn't know whether they were dead or still alive. My father begot me in fear, my mother bore me in dread. The moment I was born, I tried to turn back. I knocked at her womb and begged her to let me back in. But she wouldn't take me back because there's a severe penalty for harboring guilty people. Sometimes, when I was a baby, I suckled a sword instead of my mother's breast, and then when she gave me her breast I was afraid, I thought it was a sword. They sent me to school and I graduated with the degree of Doctor of Fear. And now I'll give you a piece of advice: Be afraid, little boy, be afraid.

BOBBIE: No, my dear sir, I'm not afraid of you.

VATZLAV: Ah, woe is me!

BOBBIE: You've had an unhappy childhood, I agree. Try not to think of it.

VATZLAV: O, wretched fate.

BOBBIE: You were unhappy, but now cheer up.

VATZLAV: O, misery, misery.

BOBBIE: Let's be friends. (*He offers to shake hands.*) Put it there.

VATZLAV: Pity, oh, have pity.

BOBBIE: Forget the past.

VATZLAV: Forget the past? Those glorious days? No one was ever beaten like me. Understand? No one. I hold the world's record for beatings and I'm proud of it. You can search the world over and you won't find anyone who can boast such beatings. No one can take the glory of my martyrdom away from me. If anyone tells me he was beaten, I'll answer that I was beaten more.

BOBBIE: I see. You want to build a monument to your degradation . . .

VATZLAV: Down on your knees to it.

BOBBIE: To make a virtue of your weakness . . .

VATZLAV: Pray to it.

BOBBIE: To find beauty in your humiliation . . .

VATZLAV: Why shouldn't I?

BOBBIE: I don't see what you're complaining about. I believe you were made to walk on all fours. With all the pleasures you seem to get out of your misery, what more do you need to make you happy?

VATZLAV: I want to be feared! Is it fair that I should be afraid of everyone and that no one should be afraid of me? No, it's not fair. There will be no justice in the world until I've scared the shit out of someone. Can't you think of someone?

BOBBIE: You mean someone weaker than you?

VATZLAV: That's right.

BOBBIE: No, I'm afraid not.

VATZLAV: Not for my own benefit . . . It's for the principle!

BOBBIE: Oh, if it's for the principle, cheer up. We'll find somebody.

VATZLAV: I like you, kid. We foreigners are tenderhearted. We like to chat, to exchange ideas. We're not stones like the curious specimens around here who'd rather die than open their mouths. We may be uncouth, but at least we're sincere. Warmhearted folk who speak their minds . . .

BOBBIE: Tell me, have you seen a child's parents around here?

VATZLAV: Honest, kindly . . .

BOBBIE (aside): Still patting himself on the back.

VATZLAV: Simple, friendly . . .

BOBBIE: I asked you a question.

VATZLAV: Come to my arms.

He embraces BOBBIE.

I'm so moved.

BOBBIE: Aren't you going to answer me?

VATZLAV: Brother, I love you.

BOBBIE: Then you've seen them?

VATZLAV: If that old skinflint and exploiter of bears is your father, I saw him going that way with his wife.

BOBBIE: Take me to them.

They exit left.

SCENE 15

Enter right QUAIL *and* SASSAFRAS.

SASSAFRAS: They say something's going to happen.
QUAIL: You think . . . pss . . . pss . . .
SASSAFRAS: Shh . . . shh . . .
QUAIL: I didn't say a word.
SASSAFRAS: You didn't say a word, but you said it mighty loud.
QUAIL: Scaredycat!
SASSAFRAS: I'm no scaredycat, but I keep my bravery to myself.
QUAIL: It seems they've seen a comet.
SASSAFRAS: Heaven help us!
QUAIL: With a long tail.
SASSAFRAS: That looks like . . .
QUAIL: Shh . . . shh . . .
SASSAFRAS: I didn't say a word.
QUAIL: But you were going to.
SASSAFRAS: All right. No tail.
QUAIL: Why no tail?
SASSAFRAS: Don't contradict me, neighbor. (*Raising his voice.*) No tail!
QUAIL: All right, all right.
SASSAFRAS (*under his breath*): Well, what about that tail?

> QUAIL *whispers in his ear.*

I don't believe it.

QUAIL: As true as I'm standing here.

SASSAFRAS: What do you think of that?

MR. BAT'S VOICE (*off stage*): Raspberries! Raspberries!

QUAIL: Of what, neighbor?

SASSAFRAS: I didn't say a word.

QUAIL: I thought you did.

SASSAFRAS: You think too much.

QUAIL: So do you.

They exit left.

SCENE 16

Enter right VATZLAV *and* BOBBIE.

VATZLAV: I'm telling you, pal, everybody loves me. The women most of all . . . The way they ran after me . . . I couldn't get rid of them . . . Some days, I remember, I used to shut myself up at home, just to be alone. I'm reading my paper and whistling—I'm musical, you see—when all of a sudden, bam! A broad flies in through the window. The poor thing was so crazy about me she jumped right in with her eyes closed. Trouble, trouble. Cost me a fortune in window panes alone. The glaziers all knew me. When they passed me on the street they'd say: "At your service, sir, any window panes today?"

BOBBIE: Climb a tree and report.

VATZLAV *climbs on Bobbie's shoulders.*

What do you see?

VATZLAV: People.

BOBBIE: What kind of people?

VATZLAV: Scum.

BOBBIE: Just plain people?

VATZLAV: Oh, oh no. There's my boss and his wife.

BOBBIE: Let me up.

> BOBBIE *climbs on* Vatzlav's *shoulders.*

Good God, what're they doing? All tangled up with the people. Feasting on the people.

VATZLAV: You'll find out.

BOBBIE: On the body of the people. His suckers are clinging to the body of the people, he's strangling them with his awful tentacles . . . Oh, Father, oh my father . . .

VATZLAV: What about your father?

BOBBIE: He's drinking the blood of the people!

VATZLAV: Nice daddy you've got there. Congratulations.

CHORUS OF THE PEOPLE (*off stage*): Drink our blood, my lord!

WOMAN'S VOICE (*off stage*): I've got a baby here, a luscious baby. Help yourself, my lord!

CHORUS OF THE PEOPLE (*off stage*): Drink up, my lord!

MAN'S VOICE (*off stage*): I'm an old man bowed with age, bled since childhood, but there's still some left.

CHORUS OF THE PEOPLE (*off stage*): Drink up, my lord!

MAN'S VOICE (*off stage*): We haven't many red corpuscles left, but you're welcome . . .

WOMAN'S VOICE (*off stage*): We beg you . . .

CHORUS OF THE PEOPLE (*off stage*): Drink our blood, my lord!

BOBBIE: Oh, Father, Father, so that's your raspberries. You never told me about your loathsome meals, your lunches, your dinners, your snacks . . .

VATZLAV: It wasn't anything to brag about.

BOBBIE: Maybe breakfast, too.

VATZLAV: Very likely.

BOBBIE: You talked about raspberries and you drank the blood of the people.

VATZLAV: There you have it.

BOBBIE: My father! A bloodsucker!

They exit right. BOBBIE *remains on Vatzlav's shoulders.*

SCENE 17

Enter left SASSAFRAS *and* QUAIL.

QUAIL: Did they suck your blood, neighbor?

SASSAFRAS: Sure did.

QUAIL: The boss sucked me dry.

SASSAFRAS: The boss is nothing. The missus is worse. When she gets her suckers into you, heaven help you.

QUAIL: Oh, well, it's all in a day's work.

SASSAFRAS: They say Jake saw Justice.

QUAIL: Where'd he see her?

SASSAFRAS: Swimming in the pond over near Gloomy Glen.

QUAIL: Naked?

SASSAFRAS: You bet. Pretty, too . . .

QUAIL: You know what, neighbor? Suppose we go over Gloomy Glen way.

SASSAFRAS: Take a look at Justice?

QUAIL: Not at frogs . . .

SASSAFRAS: You in a hurry, neighbor?

QUAIL: If Jake can see her, why can't I?

They exit right.

SCENE 18

Enter right VATZLAV *and* BOBBIE.

BOBBIE (*climbing down from Vatzlav's shoulders*): I don't want to be Mr. Bat's little boy anymore.

VATZLAV: What do you want to be?

BOBBIE: A bear.

VATZLAV: How're you gonna swing that?

BOBBIE: Let's swap. Give me your skin.

VATZLAV: What? Deny my shaggy parents? My dear old dad with his black nose and my four-footed mother? You've got the wrong guy.

BOBBIE: Dear quadruped, give me your parentage.

VATZLAV: I love them so . . .

BOBBIE: Do it for me.

VATZLAV: Let me think. Only an unworthy son renounces his parents. But an unworthy son never renounces his parents for nothing. That would be bad business. I can't let you have them for nothing, because only an unworthy son renounces his parents and if I let you have them for nothing I wouldn't be an unworthy son. Follow me?

BOBBIE: I'll give you my watch.

He gives VATZLAV *his watch.*

VATZLAV: That's different. I'm turning into an unworthy son. I can feel it.

BOBBIE: Will that do it?

VATZLAV: I'm not a hundred percent unworthy yet.

BOBBIE: Take my ring.

He gives VATZLAV *his ring.*

VATZLAV: That's for my daddy. What do I get for my mummy?

BOBBIE: I haven't got anything else.

VATZLAV: Oh, well, let's say I've sold all of daddy and only part of mummy. Maybe it's better that way. I'm not renouncing my family entirely.

He gives BOBBIE *his bear mask.*

Goodby, bear. (*He exits right.*)

BOBBIE (*putting on the mask*): Goodby, Bat family! (*He exits left.*)

SCENE 19

Enter right THE GENIUS. *He wears an antique coat and has a bushy black beard. He is bald.* JUSTINE *runs in from the left. She is a beautiful girl wearing a white muslin dress with a wreath of daisies in her hair.*

JUSTINE (*presses her head against The Genius's chest*): Oh Father, Father!

THE GENIUS: What's the matter, child?

JUSTINE: I went to the meadow to plait a wreath.

THE GENIUS: No harm in that. It's most becoming.

JUSTINE: When I'd finished, I looked at my reflection in the pond.

THE GENIUS: All perfectly innocent, so far.

JUSTINE: While I was looking at myself, a peasant came out of the bushes and gaped at me.

THE GENIUS: You can't forbid an honest peasant to look at you.

JUSTINE: But he wasn't honest.

THE GENIUS: You mustn't say that. Only the rich are dishonest, the poor are always honest.

JUSTINE: This one wasn't.

THE GENIUS: How do you know?

JUSTINE: Because when I took off my dress . . .

THE GENIUS: Oh, you took off your dress?

JUSTINE: I was going to bathe.

THE GENIUS: And then?

JUSTINE: He took out a stick and threatened me.

THE GENIUS: With a stick?

JUSTINE: Or something like it.

THE GENIUS: And then?

JUSTINE: I thought he was going to hit me, so I ran away. I hardly had time to pick up my dress.

THE GENIUS: That was naughty of you.

JUSTINE: Should I have let him hurt me?

THE GENIUS: He had no intention of hurting you.

JUSTINE: He was shaking that cruel instrument . . .

THE GENIUS: Because he was feeling happy.

JUSTINE: Swinging it in all directions . . .

THE GENIUS: Suppose he was. It's only human that when a poor devil is feeling happy and has something in his hand he shakes it.

JUSTINE: Then he wasn't going to hurt me?

THE GENIUS: Of course not.

JUSTINE: But I thought . . .

THE GENIUS: You mustn't have such thoughts, my dear.

JUSTINE: Where do babies come from?

THE GENIUS: What did you say?

JUSTINE: I'm a big girl, now, and I ought to know.

THE GENIUS: You're right, child . . . Well . . . babies
. . . from the head.

JUSTINE: Really?

THE GENIUS: By the workings of reason. The same as in nature. Look at the flowers, the little birds . . . Nature is reasonable.

JUSTINE: You're making fun of my innocence.

THE GENIUS: I begot you with my head . . .

JUSTINE (*momentarily shocked*): Oh, Daddy!

THE GENIUS: And bore you with my head. Or better still, with my reason. I am at once your father and mother.

JUSTINE: I've had no experience with these things, but I don't see how . . . With the head, by the head . . . Is it hard to do?

THE GENIUS: It all depends. Not for me, because I'm a genius, the inspired leader of mankind.

JUSTINE: Of course. There's no one as wise as you, Father . . . Or should I say "Mother"?

THE GENIUS: As you wish.

JUSTINE: I suppose I'll have to believe you. And since you're the wisest of men you must have created me for some purpose. Why did you bring me into the world?

THE GENIUS: A pertinent question. I'm glad to find you so reasonable. It proves that you really are my daughter. Know, then, that injustice governs the world.

JUSTINE: What does that mean?

THE GENIUS: Some are rich, others are poor.

JUSTINE: What has that got to do with me?

THE GENIUS: Patience! We know that everything in the world has its contrary. Consequently, if injustice exists, justice must also exist.

JUSTINE: That sounds reasonable. But does it?

THE GENIUS: No.

JUSTINE: What a shame.

THE GENIUS: But justice must exist.

JUSTINE: You just said it didn't.

THE.GENIUS: Have you forgotten reason? Thanks to reason, my child, everything can be set right, for the world is reasonable. Since justice does not exist, it must be invented. And that's why I created you, the fruit of necessity fertilized by reason.

SCENE 20

Enter right VATZLAV. *Bobbie's ring is on his finger and he wears Bobbie's watch on a chain around his neck. He eavesdrops on the conversation.*

THE GENIUS: You are Justice.

JUSTINE: And what am I supposed to do?

THE GENIUS: Exactly what you've been doing. Bathe in the pond, take your hair down at night and braid it in the morning.

JUSTINE: That's easy.

THE GENIUS: And when a poor peasant wants to look at you, let him look.

JUSTINE: His eyes were so strange . . .

THE GENIUS: And don't swaddle yourself in superfluous clothing.

JUSTINE: I always take my clothes off to bathe.

THE GENIUS: Take them off even when you're not going to bathe.

JUSTINE: Really? What for?

THE GENIUS: How shall I put it? . . . You are Justice. The sight of you arouses a noble desire for justice. Inflamed by this desire, the poor will turn against the rich and do great things. They will build a new order, and in that new order you will be queen.

JUSTINE: Queen? Oh, I'd like that.

THE GENIUS: Therefore, show yourself to the people.

JUSTINE: Oh, I will. I will.

THE GENIUS: Let them see you in all your beauty.

JUSTINE: Yes! Yes!

THE GENIUS: Until now, Mr. Bat has held the stage with his ugliness. Now, your beauty will take over.

JUSTINE *starts to undress.*

No! Don't fling off your clothes like a farm girl. Disrobe with circumspection, hesitate, make it clear that you are undressing not for the audience, but for yourself. Make some show of reluctance, as though fighting down your shame. Let your secret lewdness gain the upper hand, but very slowly. Your lewdness will be measured by the shame you overcome. Begin discreetly, unveil a little, then a little more. Stop from time to time. They'll think your reluctance is winning out, but all the while they'll be certain of the contrary. For remember this: Certainty is the strongest of lures.

JUSTINE: Don't worry. I'll drive them mad. They'll follow me to the ends of the earth.

THE GENIUS: Your frivolities will serve the cause. Meanwhile, I shall go abroad to gain allies. I shall proclaim your name to many people and they will join ranks with us. Await my return. Farewell, my daughter. (*He exits right.*)

JUSTINE: Goodby, Father. (*She exits left.*)

SCENE 21

VATZLAV: Justice? I've heard of her, but this is the first time I've seen her face to face. Well, let's see what's in it for me. (*He exits left.*)

SCENE 22

Enter right SASSAFRAS *and* QUAIL.

QUAIL: Say, where is this Gloomy Glen?

SASSAFRAS: It can't be far.

QUAIL: How do you know?

SASSAFRAS: 'Cause if it's far, we've taken the wrong path.

QUAIL: You know what, neighbor Sassafras? Something tells me that if it's the wrong path we ought to turn around.

SASSAFRAS: Think so?

QUAIL: Why should we go the wrong way?

SASSAFRAS: All right, we'll turn around.

> *They do so.*

> Is it still far?

QUAIL: It depends. If we're going the right way now, it can't be far. If we're not, contrariwise.

SASSAFRAS: You know what, neighbor Quail? Something tells me we ought to turn around.

QUAIL: What makes you say that?

SASSAFRAS: 'Cause if one direction is wrong, the other must be right.

QUAIL: You've got something there.

They turn around again.

Neighbor!

SASSAFRAS: What?

QUAIL: Supposing the other's right and this way's wrong?

SASSAFRAS: Holy mackerel!

QUAIL: I'll tell you what, Sassafras. Let's go arm in arm.

SASSAFRAS: What for?

QUAIL: 'Cause supposing I was going the wrong way and you were going the right way, you'd lead me the right way. And supposing I was going the right way and you were going the wrong way, I'd hold you back.

SASSAFRAS: Good idea!

They walk arm in arm.

QUAIL: This way.

SASSAFRAS: No, that way.

QUAIL: Neighbor, seems to me you're going wrong.

SASSAFRAS: It seems to me *you're* going wrong.

QUAIL: I'm right and you're wrong.

SASSAFRAS: You must be blind.

QUAIL: Who's blind?

SASSAFRAS: You.

QUAIL: Then you're a chipmunk.

SASSAFRAS: A chipmunk?

QUAIL: Well, if you're not a chipmunk you're an ass.

SASSAFRAS: What's that again?

QUAIL: I say you're stupid, neighbor.

SASSAFRAS: And you're a baboon.

QUAIL: What?

SASSAFRAS: You heard me.

QUAIL (*imitates the braying of an ass*): Hee-haw, hee-haw!

They rush at each other and fight.

SCENE 23

Enter right BOBBIE *with the bear mask on his face. He carries writing materials.*

BOBBIE: Have you seen the boss' son?

SASSAFRAS: I've seen a baboon.

He beats QUAIL.

QUAIL: I've seen an ass.

He beats SASSAFRAS.

BOBBIE: They haven't seen me. That's fine. It proves my disguise is effective and no one recognizes me. This is a new life. Oh, how beautiful it is to begin a new life, to strip off the past. It's true I haven't had much of a past, but what there was of it was so degrading . . . Oh, there seems to be some disagreement between you two. What are you fighting about?

SASSAFRAS *and* QUAIL (*in unison*): Justice!

BOBBIE: An excellent cause. Justice is worthy of every sacrifice. But why should you fight?

QUAIL (*hitting* SASSAFRAS): Because he's an ass.

BOBBIE: I infer that you yourself are not an ass, because members of the same family don't fight among themselves. That's why I've become a bear, so I could fight the Bats. Who are you?

SASSAFRAS (*hitting* QUAIL): Baboon!

BOBBIE: Are you hitting him because he's a baboon or because you're an ass?

QUAIL: Hear that? Answer the gentleman, you ass!

SASSAFRAS: I'm hitting him because I'm *not* an ass.

BOBBIE: That's odd. I could see the point if you *were* an ass.

QUAIL *gets the upper hand. He sits on* SASSAFRAS *and beats him.*

What about you? Why are you hitting him?

QUAIL: Because I'm not a baboon.

BOBBIE: Then maybe you're an ass and he's a baboon? Speak up. Let's get to the bottom of this.

QUAIL: No, he's an ass.

BOBBIE: Then you must be the baboon.

SASSAFRAS: See? What did I tell you?

QUAIL: I'm Quail.

SASSAFRAS: And I'm Sassafras.

They stop fighting.

BOBBIE: Then where are the animals you were talking about just now? Never mind. Weren't you headed for a certain place where Justice is said to have appeared?

QUAIL *and* SASSAFRAS (*in unison*): Yes, sir.

BOBBIE: Then my advice to you is to get going. Don't waste your time arguing who's an ass and who's a baboon. Leave that to the bear, who has his own opinion. Hurry, because I'm confident that when you poor yokels reach your destination your lives will be changed. Justice will make men of you even if what Sassafras says of Quail and Quail says of Sassafras is true.

QUAIL: What do you think, neighbor?

SASSAFRAS: That's no ordinary bear. He's educated.

QUAIL: Yeah.

SASSAFRAS: He talks like a minister.

QUAIL: Yeah, he ain't the same bear. He wasn't so smart when I saw him the other day.

SASSAFRAS: Maybe he's been going to school.

SASSAFRAS *and* QUAIL *exit left.*

SCENE 24

Enter right VATZLAV.

VATZLAV (*seeing* BOBBIE *in his bear costume*): Oooh! (*He starts to run away.*)

BOBBIE: Wait!

VATZLAV: I'm not so dumb.

BOBBIE (*removing his mask*): Don't you recognize your old friend?

VATZLAV: Oh, it's you. Thank God. I thought it was me.

BOBBIE: Are you afraid of yourself?

VATZLAV: You can't imagine how terrifying I am. I know myself.

BOBBIE: But you sold me your skin. Don't you remember?

VATZLAV: I've been so upset.

BOBBIE: I can see that. What's wrong?

VATZLAV: Too much on my mind.

BOBBIE: What have you been doing with yourself?

VATZLAV: Not much. But I've got something cooking now. If it works out I'll buy you a drink.

BOBBIE: Buy me one now.

VATZLAV: It's not in the bag yet. (*He makes a move to leave.*)

BOBBIE: You're leaving?

VATZLAV: I'm in a hurry.

BOBBIE: I need you. Could you deliver a letter for me?

VATZLAV: I've got this deal . . .

BOBBIE: It won't run away.

VATZLAV: Business waits for no man. Be good. (*He exits left.*)

SCENE 25

BOBBIE (*puts on his mask and writes*): "Dear Mummy . . . " No, not Mummy. I'm a bear now. She's not my mother any more. "Dear Madam. The writer of this letter was your son, but he was devoured by a bear. I am no longer your son, I am a wild, free, and independent bear. If you wish to see me, I shall be in the forest waiting for you. Your bear."

OEDIPUS (*off stage*): I watch . . . I watch . . .

BOBBIE: That's Oedipus, my father's flunky and spy. Luckily, he's blind. Yoo-hoo! Here I am!

SCENE 26

Enter right OEDIPUS, *curly beard, Greek toga, blind man's white cane.*

OEDIPUS (*groping around with his cane*): Where?

BOBBIE (*taking him by the hand*): Here.

OEDIPUS: What are you doing?

BOBBIE: Writing a letter.

OEDIPUS: To whom?

BOBBIE: My mother.

OEDIPUS: Let me read it. (*He takes the letter and turns it in all directions.*) I don't see very well. Read it to me.

BOBBIE (*takes the letter and reads*): "Dear Madam, wife of my beloved father. I regret to inform you that I love him much more than I love you. Kindly assure him of my profound respect and affection. I belong to him alone. His obedient servant and son."

OEDIPUS: I will deliver it.

BOBBIE: I hate to inconvenience you.

OEDIPUS: Give me that letter right now!

BOBBIE: As you wish.

OEDIPUS: I watch . . . I watch . . . (*He exits right with the letter.*)

SCENE 27

BOBBIE: Now he's sure to deliver my letter. (*He exits left.*)

SCENE 28

Enter right MRS. BAT *wearing a rose corsage. She holds a fan and pulls a meticulously clipped black poodle—a toy dog on wheels—by a string. On its neck is a silver bell and a red*

bow; its paws are adorned with little red bows as is its tail;
a red cap sits on its head.

MRS. BAT: Little cutesy. Pretty doggy-woggy. Tell me, little
cutesy, do you love your mistress? Do you like her a
teensy-weensy bit? No, little cutesy doesn't love her.
Naughty, naughty, naughty. I'm angry with doggy-
woggy. Bad, bad horrid doggy-woggy. Your mistress is
angry. She's going to leave you. (*She goes to one side.*)
Is doggy-woggy sad now? That's what he gets for not
loving his mistress. It's all his fault. Ohhh. Is little cutesy
crying? (*She comes back to it.*) Don't be sad. Your
mistress forgives you. Look, she's right here. Please
don't cry. You'll break her heart. Oh, please stop, it was
all in fun. Come, little cutesy, come to mummy. (*She
rocks it in her arms.*) Good little doggy-woggy. Mummy
loves her good little, dear little doggy-woggy. Here, let
me tickle you to make you laugh. Now what! Oh, you
fresh thing! (*She puts the toy dog down.*) Now listen to
me! You belong to mummy and you've got to do what
she says. Come here! (*She pulls the dog towards her
and puts the fan in its mouth.*) Sit up! (*She threatens
it with her finger.*) You do as I say or it's all over between us. Did you think I'd let you get away with such
insolence? (*She stamps her foot.*) So, doggy-woggy
thought he could get fresh with mummy! (*Pause. She
pets it.*) Nice little doggy-woggy. Good little doggy-
woggy. Cunning little doggy-woggy. (*Losing patience.*)
So pretty! So well-behaved! (*Angry.*) Oh! Oh! So well-
behaved! (*She screams.*) Why are you so well-behaved?
(*She bursts into tears.*) Always the same, always the
same . . . Obedient, polite, cunning. It's driving me
crazy . . . (*Furious.*) Why don't you say something?
Stupid dog, why don't you say something?

SCENE 29

Enter right OEDIPUS *with the letter.*

OEDIPUS: Where are you, madam?
MRS. BAT: I'm not here.
OEDIPUS: I have a letter for you.
MRS. BAT: Here I am! (*She takes the letter and reads it.*)
    Heavens!
OEDIPUS: Yes, madam, yes, yes. That's how it is. Now, what
    do you think? . . . I can't hear you, madam.
MRS. BAT (*to herself*): A bear?
OEDIPUS: Who?
MRS. BAT: Nobody. (*She exits left, pulling the toy dog.*)

SCENE 30

OEDIPUS: What bear? (*He exits right.*)

SCENE 31

Enter right SASSAFRAS *and* QUAIL.

QUAIL (*limping*): If this goes on, neighbor, justice can lick my ass. I got a blister on my left foot and I can feel one coming on my right foot if we don't find her pretty soon.

SCENE 32

Enter left VATZLAV. *He wears, over his shirt, a loud, yellow blazer with silver trimming, in glaring contrast to his shirt, ragged trousers, and heavy wooden clogs. He also wears a bowler, Bobbie's ring and watch.*

VATZLAV: Well, gentlemen, you've come to the right place.
QUAIL (*to* SASSAFRAS): Gentlemen? Does he mean us?
SASSAFRAS: Must be some mistake.
VATZLAV: No mistake. The customer's always right and that makes him a gentleman.
QUAIL: You're very kind, sir. . . Who are you?
VATZLAV (*bowing*): An artist.

QUAIL: Then you're a nice artist. But we're looking for a certain person that Jake saw by the pond in Gloomy Glen. Have you seen her?

VATZLAV: She's right here. Be seated, gentlemen.

QUAIL: Do you see her, Sassafras?

SASSAFRAS (*with dignity*): *Mister* Sassafras!

QUAIL: I don't see a thing. Let us pass, sir. We got no time to lose.

VATZLAV: There she is. (*He points left.*)

SASSAFRAS *moves to the left.*

QUAIL: Hiding right there? Who'd have thought it? God bless you, sir . . . Hey, where you going, neighbor Sassafras?

SASSAFRAS (*with dignity*): *Mister* Sassafras.

QUAIL (*barring the way*): Let me go first.

SASSAFRAS (*haughtily*): Beg your pardon, Quail. I go first.

QUAIL: I go first.

They jostle each other.

VATZLAV: Don't push, gentlemen. Pay your money and there'll be room for everybody.

QUAIL: Money? Jake saw her for free.

VATZLAV: Because if you pay, we all stand to gain. If it's free, nobody gains but you. And justice means equal gain for all. Don't be unjust when you're looking for justice.

SASSAFRAS: She was supposed to be in Gloomy Glen, down by the pond.

VATZLAV: Ah, rustic simplicity. Do you think justice grows in the swamps like rushes? Do you think she wades knee-deep in water like a heron? No, my simple-minded friends. Justice is a product not of nature but of reason. She is a delicate creature prone to pneumonia.

And just for your convenience you want her to appear
under the open sky, in the wind and rain, in ice and
in snow? And for nothing! You ought to be ashamed
of yourselves! Goodby!

QUAIL: Do we pay, neighbor?

SASSAFRAS: Maybe he'll give us a discount.

VATZLAV: You still here?

QUAIL: He won't come down.

SASSAFRAS: All right, we'll pay.

They pay VATZLAV.

VATZLAV (*pocketing the money*): You're in luck. I'm giving
you the last two seats.

VATZLAV, SASSAFRAS, *and* QUAIL *exit left.*

SCENE 33

Enter left MRS. BAT *pulling the toy dog which holds her fan
in its mouth.*

MRS. BAT (*to the dog*): I dreamt I was going through the
woods. Suddenly you jumped out of the bushes. Your
jaws were wide open and you had terrible, white fangs.
I ran away and came to a clearing. In the clearing there
was an enormous spit. My husband was turning it. He
was wearing a chef's hat and he said: "He's turning
red. He tastes best when he's red." And you were on
the spit. I didn't want to eat you, but you came running
after me. I'm lost, I thought, unless I can escape into
my own belly. Then . . . (*Screams.*) How dare you

suspect me? Take it back! You're nasty, disgusting, shameless. Do you realize what you're accusing me of? Is that what you've been thinking? At last I've had a glimpse of your sick brain. You vicious little brat. How dare you be jealous of your own fiendish imagination? You've insulted me. That's enough. Not another word. I won't listen to your ravings. I forbid you. Think what you please, but leave me out of it . . . I'm not talking to you. (*She turns her back to the toy dog.*) Oh, no. Certainly not. (*After each sentence she pauses, as if listening to the toy dog's answer.*) Really? . . . That's odd . . . As you wish . . . No . . . No, I don't know him . . . I've never laid eyes on him . . . Ah, what's that? . . . What bear? . . . Well, what of it? . . . Do you want me to swear? . . . As you wish . . . All right, I swear. Now are you satisfied? . . . Starting in again? . . . I've just told you . . . What more do you want to know? . . . I've told you everything . . . That's enough . . . I'm tired . . . Oh, leave me alone . . . Stop, stop . . . I've had enough . . . What *do* you want? . . . I refuse to answer. You bore me . . . What? . . . You've been spying on me . . . You're vile, vile. You dared! . . . Serves you right. It's your own fault . . . Yes, yes, yes, can I help it if you're not a bear? . . . I love him! . . . Since when? From the very first moment . . . No, go away. It's all over between us . . . No, it's no use . . . Ha, ha! You, a bear? Don't even try. You're pathetic . . . Don't beg me, don't apologize, you're wasting your time . . . You won't? Then don't! (*She snatches her fan from the toy dog's mouth.*) I'm going away. (*She takes a few steps, pulling the toy dog along.*) Don't follow me . . . You still here? . . . You threaten me? . . . Brute force? . . . Let me go! . . .

Take your paws off me! . . . Nothing can stop me!
. . . I never want to see you again, understand? Nasty
beast! (*She kicks the toy dog and drops the leash.*) But
don't forget the beauty of the fading rose. I'll leave you
a memento. (*She takes a rose from her corsage and
throws it at the toy dog.*) Be faithful to it. (*She exits
right. A moment later the toy dog is slowly pulled after
her.*)

SCENE 34

A drum is heard. A small curtain drops from the flies.
VATZLAV *enters right beating a drum hanging from his neck.*
QUAIL *and* SASSAFRAS *follow.*

VATZLAV: Here we are. Be seated, gentlemen, be seated. In
a few moments Justice will appear.

QUAIL *and* SASSAFRAS *sit down side by side in front of
the small curtain with their backs to the audience.*

Anyone else? Anyone else? A golden opportunity. Step
in, step right in.

SCENE 35

Enter right MR. BAT.

MR. BAT: I want a seat in the orchestra.

VATZLAV (*running up to him, eagerly*): Certainly, your Excellency. We have the best seat in the house for you.

He leads MR. BAT *toward center stage and kicks* SASSAFRAS *and* QUAIL.

Hey, you, a seat for his Excellency!

SASSAFRAS *and* QUAIL *get down on all fours, side by side, facing the audience.* VATZLAV *wipes off their backs with his sleeve, as though dusting a chair.*

Here you are, your Excellency. I think you'll be comfortable.

QUAIL: What about us?

SASSAFRAS *puts his hand over Quail's mouth.* MR. BAT *sits down on them facing the curtain, his back to the audience.*

VATZLAV: Your attention, please!

He beats his drum. The curtain rises just enough to show JUSTINE *in the costume of a strip-tease artist.*

Men are born and always continue free and equal. Civil distinctions, therefore, can be given only for public service.

QUAIL: Can you see anything, neighbor Sassafras?

SASSAFRAS: Nope.

QUAIL: Me neither.

VATZLAV (*stops beating the drum*): What's the disturbance?

QUAIL: It ain't us. We're chairs.

VATZLAV: I beg your pardon, your Excellency. That chair squeaks.

> VATZLAV *goes over to* QUAIL *and kicks him. He beats his drum and continues his declamation while* JUSTINE *undresses in the classical strip-tease style.*

> The end of all political associations is the preservation of natural and unalienable rights of man. And these rights are liberty, property, security, and resistance of oppression . . .

QUAIL: Say, man's got it good.

SASSAFRAS (*sighing*): Yeah, wouldn't you like to be him?

VATZLAV: Liberty consists of the power to do whatever does not injure others. The exercise of the natural rights of every man has no limit other than those which are necessary to secure to every other man the free exercise of the same rights . . .

QUAIL: Punch me in the jaw, neighbor.

SASSAFRAS: Why, neighbor?

QUAIL: So I can punch you back.

SASSAFRAS: Oh, that's different.

> SASSAFRAS *punches* QUAIL; QUAIL *punches* SASSAFRAS.

VATZLAV: The law ought to prohibit only actions harmful to society. What is not prohibited by the law should not be hindered . . .

> SASSAFRAS *picks his nose.*

QUAIL: Sassafras, take your finger out of your nose!

SASSAFRAS: It's my nose, ain't it? Is it hurting you?

QUAIL: It don't hurt me none, but it looks bad.

SASSAFRAS: It's my right.

VATZLAV: And no man can be compelled to do what the law does not expressly prohibit . . .

QUAIL: But nobody's making you.

SASSAFRAS: All right, I'll stop. (*He stops picking his nose.*)

VATZLAV: The law is an expression of the will of the community. All citizens have a right to concur, either personally or by their representatives, in its formation. It should be the same to all, whether it protects or punishes; and all being equal in its sight, are equally eligible to all honors, places, and employment . . . No man ought to be molested on account of his opinions, not even on account of his religious opinions, provided his practice of them does not disturb the public order.

SASSAFRAS: Shit!

VATZLAV *stops beating the drum and* JUSTINE *stops undressing.*

VATZLAV (*severely*): Is that a thought or an opinion?

SASSAFRAS: We-ell . . .

QUAIL: He didn't really mean it.

VATZLAV (*resumes beating the drum*): The unrestrained communication of thought and opinion being one of the most estimable rights of man, every citizen may speak, write, and publish freely. (*He stops beating. To* SASSAFRAS.) If it's a thought or an opinion you're expressing, okay. But if it's just plain shit . . .

QUAIL: Which is it, Sassafras?

SASSAFRAS: Shit.

VATZLAV (*to* QUAIL): Is he an anarchist?

QUAIL: Hell, no. He's cracked.

VATZLAV: We'll see about that.

He continues beating the drum as JUSTINE *resumes her strip tease.*

Every man is innocent until proven guilty. But if jail is necessary, all unnecessary discomfort and severity should be prohibited by law.

JUSTINE *completes her strip tease and takes her final pose.* MR. BAT *applauds. The curtain falls, concealing* JUSTINE. VATZLAV *bows as if the applause was meant for him.* MR. BAT *exits right.*

SCENE 36

SASSAFRAS *and* QUAIL *rise, holding each other up.* QUAIL *limps.*

SASSAFRAS: What's the matter, neighbor Quail?
QUAIL: I've got blisters.
VATZLAV: The rights to property being inviolable and sacred, no one ought to be deprived of them except in cases of clear public necessity, legally ascertained, and on condition of a previous just indemnity.

SASSAFRAS *and* QUAIL *exit right.* QUAIL *limps along. The small curtain disappears into the flies.* VATZLAV *follows the peasants.* JUSTINE *exits left.*

SCENE 37

Enter right THE GENIUS *and* THE GUIDE.

THE GUIDE: This is as far as I can go.

THE GENIUS: Lead me to the other side of the hill. I can find my own way after that.

THE GUIDE: No, I can go no further.

THE GENIUS: Why not?

THE GUIDE: Because the crest of the hill is the border. On the other side, they have orders to castrate all camels.

THE GENIUS: But you're not a camel!

THE GUIDE: It's obvious that you're a stranger to these parts. First they castrate, then they look to see if you're a camel.

THE GENIUS: Why was such an order given?

THE GUIDE: Because it's easier to cut things off than to make them grow.

THE GENIUS: They're right. A camel's possessions are his private property and private property is the curse of society.

THE GUIDE: That's it, sir. And once deprived of his private property, the camel is able to hit high notes he would never have attempted before.

THE GENIUS: Then, surely, he sings hymns to the glory of justice.

A solemn cantata is heard sung by men with high falsetto voices.

THE GUIDE: Here they come. (*He runs off left.*)

THE GENIUS: I will follow those voices. Guide my steps, sweet music. (*He exits right.*)

SCENE 38

Enter right MRS. BAT *carrying an earthenware pot.*

MRS. BAT: I'm in love with the bear. There's no cure for it and I don't want one. If I had a cure, I'd throw it away. I'd burn this whole forest if it contained a balm that could heal my heart. I myself am my sickness. I would die if I were cured. My conscience sermonizes me, but I've left it at home. It's a conscience for home use, and this is the wilderness. What is forbidden in the city is permitted in the forest. The forest is without sin. How can there be sin where there are no men, but only bears?

OEDIPUS (*off stage*): Wait for me, madam.

MRS. BAT: He's found me, after all.

SCENE 39

Enter right OEDIPUS.

OEDIPUS: Where are you, madam?

MRS. BAT: Here. (*She walks to the other side of the stage.*)

OEDIPUS (*goes to where she was before; he pokes around with his cane*): You're not here at all.

MRS. BAT: Not there. Here.

OEDIPUS *goes towards the voice.* MRS. BAT *goes back to where she was before.*

OEDIPUS: She says here when she's there. And when I go there, she's here.

MRS. BAT: Not there.

She takes OEDIPUS *by the hand and leads him to where she was before.*

Here!

OEDIPUS: Oh, here.

MRS. BAT: Here. (*Surprised.*) Why, yes, I must have been mistaken.

OEDIPUS (*tapping the pot gently with his cane*): What have you got there, madam?

MRS. BAT (*hiding the pot behind her back*): Nothing.

OEDIPUS: In that little pot?

MRS. BAT: Nothing.

OEDIPUS: Then what do you need the pot for?

MRS. BAT: It's a pot full of nothing.

OEDIPUS: Let me taste it.

MRS. BAT: But it's a bitter nothing.

OEDIPUS (*menacingly*): I wish to taste it, madam.

She offers him the pot. He puts his finger into the pot and licks his finger.

Mmm . . . it's sweet.

MRS. BAT: It's bitter.

OEDIPUS: It's honey, madam.

MRS. BAT: Oh. Then it must be sweet.

OEDIPUS: Taking honey to the forest? That's dangerous.

MRS. BAT: Who would harm me?
OEDIPUS: The bears.
MRS. BAT: Who're they?
OEDIPUS: They love honey.
MRS. BAT: Really? I didn't know.

SCENE 40

Enter left BOBBIE *wearing his bear mask. He is not seen by the others.*

OEDIPUS: What is the reason, madam, for this strange excursion?
MRS. BAT: I wanted to take a walk.
OEDIPUS: All alone?
MRS. BAT: Do you know someone who can do my breathing for me?
OEDIPUS: At this time of day?
MRS. BAT: I need air at all hours. It's best at dusk.
OEDIPUS: It will soon be night.
MRS. BAT (*retreating slowly to the left, on tiptoe*): Night? What's that to me?
OEDIPUS: Don't trifle with darkness, madam. The forest is always dangerous, but it's most dangerous at night.
MRS. BAT: I fear neither the forest nor the darkness. Why should I?
OEDIPUS: Because in the darkness good is indistinguishable from evil.
MRS. BAT: That's fine. If I can't see evil, it won't tempt me.

OEDIPUS: It's not fine at all. In the darkness you can sin without knowing it.

MRS. BAT: I don't want to know. (*She exits left.*)

SCENE 41

OEDIPUS: Oh, madam, madam. I once sinned without knowing it. I was punished with blindness.

BOBBIE: Why were you punished if you didn't know?

OEDIPUS: Because the law is the law. Because I had eyes and I acted like a blind man, I was made blind. Now I'm the guardian of the law.

BOBBIE: What's the good of the law?

OEDIPUS: To safeguard morality.

BOBBIE: What's the good of morality?

OEDIPUS: Our morality is the basis of our civilization.

BOBBIE: But supposing it were the other way around. Suppose our civilization is the basis of our morality.

OEDIPUS: Our morality would be a necessity, hence all the more justified.

BOBBIE: Then it's moral for my father to drink the blood of the people in broad daylight. If that's morality, the civilization it's based on should rot. No, the morality such a civilization is based on should rot. Or, damn it, let them both rot.

OEDIPUS: What's that you're saying, madam . . . Is that your voice?

BOBBIE: No, it's mine.

OEDIPUS: Oh. Then it's a voice that resembles another as a mother's voice resembles a child's.

BOBBIE: Tell me how you sinned.

OEDIPUS: I killed my father and committed incest with my mother.

BOBBIE: Good for you. (*He exits left.*)

SCENE 42

OEDIPUS: Who said that? (*He gropes around with his cane and exits left.*)

SCENE 43

Enter right SASSAFRAS *and* QUAIL *carrying* VATZLAV *in a litter made up of an ornate armchair slung on two long poles.* QUAIL *limps.*

VATZLAV: These damn woods. They may be all right for animals but not for honest citizens who've made a little money by the sweat of their brows. What do you find in woods like these? Bears and bandits. The former set a bad example because they don't work and own no property. That's how they show it's possible to get along without doing anything or owning anything. As for the bandits, let's not tempt fate by even mentioning them. There've been a lot of strangers hanging around here lately, tramps from God knows where, attracted by the wealth and freedom of our country.

Runaway slaves. Looking for freedom. That's what they say. But I say each man gets only as much freedom as he deserves. Why were they slaves in their own country if they deserved better?

QUAIL *stumbles.*

Watch your step!

QUAIL: My foot hurts.

VATZLAV: Who cares?

QUAIL: Don't say that, boss. If all men are equal, my foot's as good as yours.

SASSAFRAS: You've got to be nice to us because we're "the people."

VATZLAV: What makes you so smart all of a sudden?

SASSAFRAS: It was in the paper.

VATZLAV (*to* SASSAFRAS): That's the times for you. Now that they've invented justice, everybody's talking about Quail. Quail is suffering, so you've got to suffer, too. You can't even sleep or eat in peace. If you sleep they tell you: "Don't sleep, Quail isn't sleeping." If you eat, they say: "Don't eat, Quail isn't eating." The sun sets. "Don't set, Mr. Sun, Quail isn't setting." A tree blossoms. "Stop blossoming, Mr. Tree, Quail isn't blossoming." To hell with you and your blossoms.

QUAIL: Don't curse, sir. I don't mind, but if society heard you they wouldn't like it.

VATZLAV: I'm not afraid of the truth. A fish used to be a fish, a poor man used to be a poor man. When you ate fish, the poor man stood and watched you. Now it's all mixed up. The fish is still a fish, but the poor man is a bone and he sticks in your throat.

SASSAFRAS: That's not the whole of it, boss. They say the fish will eat us all soon, you and us and them.

VATZLAV: The fish? What fish?

SASSAFRAS: The fish Leviathan.
QUAIL: The end of the world.
VATZLAV: When? Now? Just when business was beginning to look up?

SASSAFRAS *and* QUAIL, *carrying* VATZLAV, *exit left.*

SCENE 44

Enter right MRS. BAT *with her pot of honey.*

MRS. BAT: My idiotic conscience has warned me of the night. What difference does it make whether I see what I'm doing? Besides, I have no intention of sinning. If I were going to sin, I'd feel ashamed, I'd hide. If I had evil thoughts, I'd hide my honey. But I'm not hiding it and that means I'm above suspicion. If I had anything to hide, I wouldn't cry aloud in the forest; I wouldn't tempt the hungry bear. But instead, I shout: "Honey! Honey! Come and get it!" (*She exits left.*)

SCENE 45

Enter right QUAIL *and* SASSAFRAS *carrying* VATZLAV *in the litter.*

VATZLAV: How can you tell when it's the end of the world?
SASSAFRAS: First it gets very dark.

VATZLAV: It's getting dark now.

QUAIL: It's not really dark now. The moon is rising.

VATZLAV: That's good news.

SASSAFRAS: There'll be plenty of light.

VATZLAV: Give me darkness. I wish the moon would go out.

QUAIL: It's not really light, boss. That's not the moon. It's somebody coming with a candle.

SCENE 46

Enter right OEDIPUS *with a lighted candle.*

OEDIPUS: Night has fallen. Anything can happen in the darkness. I've lighted my candle to prevent conscience from falling asleep. Because I know by sad experience how easy it is to sin even with seeing eyes. In the dusk it's easier still, and for sinning the black night is the best time of all.

VATZLAV: A bandit. All shaggy . . . with evil in his eyes
. . .

SASSAFRAS *and* QUAIL *drop the litter and fall on their knees before* OEDIPUS.

SASSAFRAS *and* QUAIL (*in unison*): O, saint!

VATZLAV: A saint? Damn near broke my neck with his saint-liness. Looks more like a beggar to me. Hey, you! No begging around here!

QUAIL (*to* OEDIPUS): Your blessing.

VATZLAV: Forget it.

OEDIPUS (*walks slowly to the left, tapping his cane on the ground*): I can tell by the voices that here are two pious men and one cheapskate. But none of these voices is the voice of that wicked man or that godless woman. I will go my way.

SASSAFRAS (*rising from his knees*): He won't give us his blessing.

VATZLAV: He walks like a blind man. But why should a blind man carry a lighted candle? (*To* OEDIPUS.) Hey! What are you doing with a candle if you're blind?

OEDIPUS: This candle, sir, protects us all against evil.

VATZLAV: Either he's pretending to be blind, and then he's a crook, or he's really blind, and then he's off his rocker.

OEDIPUS: Woe betide us if it goes out.

VATZLAV: We'll see about that! (*He blows the candle out.*)

OEDIPUS: Shine, candle, shine! (*He exits left.*)

SCENE 47

VATZLAV: A lunatic. I knew there were bandits and bears in these woods . . . I'd forgotten about lunatics. What's the matter with you two? You look like door posts.

SASSAFRAS (*genuflecting*): You blew the saint's candle out!

VATZLAV: So what?

QUAIL (*genuflecting*): Woe is us!

VATZLAV: Have you both gone crazy?

QUAIL *and* SASSAFRAS *run out right.*

Hey . . . stop . . . wait for me . . . Is everybody nuts? (*He hoists the litter on his back and runs after them.*)

SCENE 48

Enter left MR. BAT *followed by* THE LACKEY.

MR. BAT: What seems to be the trouble?

THE LACKEY: In the first place, madam is very much upset.

MR. BAT: And in the second place?

THE LACKEY: It seems that the bear is stirring up trouble. He's been speaking to the peasants, inciting them to rebel.

MR. BAT: Tell the foresters to get ready for the hunt. Tell them to round up the hounds and load the guns.

THE LACKEY *exits left.*

SCENE 49

Enter right the toy dog.

MR. BAT: What do you want, you toady? Can't you keep an eye on your mistress? Do you think I feed you to run loose like a mutt? Go find her or I'll make you a watch-dog, and all you'll get to eat is what you can bite out of trespassers. Where's your mistress? You're plotting something, you black bastard. What woods? . . . Why in the woods? . . . Shh . . . Not so loud . . .

Dog, curly courtesan, quadruped page, flatterer, tail wagger, loathsome mongrel! If your perfumed snout isn't lying I'll reward you with his bones, and a bear has plenty. You'll be gnawing on them all winter. And his skin, I'll give you his skin for a bed. But if you've lied . . . (*He picks up the toy dog and shakes it.*) You'll be sorry, Iago.

He tosses the dog off stage right. He claps his hands and THE LACKEY *enters.*

Call the hunt!

MR. BAT *and* THE LACKEY *exit left.*

SCENE 50

Enter right QUAIL *and* SASSAFRAS *looking at the sky.*

SASSAFRAS: That's funny. Not a cloud in the sky and it's dark. It's a long way till night and the stars are shining.

QUAIL *blows his nose loudly. A flash of lightning.*

Better cut that out, neighbor.
QUAIL: What did I do?
SASSAFRAS: I dunno. Maybe you're only blowing your nose, but maybe you're thundering, too, and that makes for lightning.

QUAIL *blows his nose twice. Two flashes of lightning.*

Cut it out!
QUAIL: Man!

SASSAFRAS: What did I tell you?

QUAIL: Beats the shit out of me.

SASSAFRAS: Don't worry. There's plenty left.

QUAIL: You know what, neighbor? I'll try it again.

SASSAFRAS: No, don't.

> QUAIL *blows his nose once. They wait. No lightning.*

QUAIL: Hey, no lightning.

SASSAFRAS: Nope.

QUAIL: But it's getting darker.

> A *violent flash of lightning followed by three claps of thunder.* QUAIL *and* SASSAFRAS *run to the other side of the stage and hold their ears.*

SASSAFRAS: Quit it, neighbor.

> A *fourth explosion, louder than the others.*

> Cut it out, I tell you.

QUAIL: It ain't me. It's him up there.

SASSAFRAS: I don't believe you. I'll never believe you again.

> QUAIL *and* SASSAFRAS *run out left.*

SCENE 51

A pack of dogs barking, seemingly getting closer. VATZLAV *runs in from the right with the litter on his back. His violent movements indicate that he is being attacked by the pack. He struggles, kicks, rushes forward, snatches first one of his legs and then the other from the imaginary dogs.*

VATZLAV: Get away! Don't touch me! It's all a mistake, Mr.
Hound. I'm a law-abiding citizen . . . I pay my taxes
. . . Ouch! Let go, you mutt . . . That's my leg.
Why does the government hire such stupid mongrels?
. . . Ouch! . . . Ouch! . . . I was joking, nice dog.
Hunting's all right with me if you hunt the right peo-
ple. I'm all for it . . . Get away, you mutt, beat it
. . . No, he won't . . . Not my ears! Please stick to
my legs . . . Ouch! . . . Ouch! . . . Get away, you
mutts. No, I didn't mean you, you noble descendants
of the great whale . . . I'll put in a complaint. You'll
see . . . I've got witnesses . . . I've got friends . . .
I've got justice on my side! . . . Ouch! . . . Ouch!
. . . I've got children! (*He runs out left as the barking recedes and dies away.*)

SCENE 52

Enter right OEDIPUS *and* BOBBIE. BOBBIE *is wearing his bear
mask.* OEDIPUS *is walking backwards.* BOBBIE *is holding the
point of his sword at Oedipus's throat.*

BOBBIE: Defend yourself!
OEDIPUS: If you have a conscience . . .
BOBBIE: Defend yourself!
OEDIPUS: I will not defend myself, sir, I will defend the
law . . .
BOBBIE: Defend yourself!

They assume the stance of fencers. OEDIPUS *awkwardly
crosses his white cane with Bobbie's sword.* BOBBIE

could easily strike the cane from the blind man's hand but he seems to derive pleasure from his superiority. He repeatedly allows OEDIPUS *to recover his guard, then attacks again and knocks the cane aside, laughing. Still fencing, they exit right.*

SCENE 53

The barking of dogs is heard. VATZLAV *runs in from the right with his litter on his back. He is out of breath. He puts the litter on the ground and sits down in the chair to catch his breath.*

VATZLAV: Come to think of it, they're right. Animals are smart. They smelled a foreigner. Who should they bite? Not one of their own people! If I were in their place, I'd start with myself, too, and leave the natives for later. But that's no help because I'm not in their place. (*The barking gets louder.*) Christ, here they come again. (*He puts the litter on his back and runs off left.*)

SCENE 54

Enter right BOBBIE *wearing his mask and* MR. BAT. *They fight violently with their swords.* MR. BAT *is obviously the stronger of the two and* BOBBIE *retreats. They exit left, fighting.*

SCENE 55

Enter right THE LACKEY, *running.*

THE LACKEY: Master! Master! (*He runs out left.*)

SCENE 56

Enter right MRS. BAT *dressed as a comic-opera gypsy. She holds a tambourine which she shakes during her speech.*

MRS. BAT: I'll teach my bear to dance and we'll go everywhere together. We'll go from city to city. The good folk won't refuse us their charity. We'll go to baptisms and weddings, dances and fairs. But we'll keep away from funerals, fires, and public executions. We'll steer clear of churches, cathedrals, and convents because the Church doesn't approve of us. We'll avoid legislatures, judges, court houses, and district attorneys, in short, all people and institutions engaged in making laws or enforcing them. We'll avoid devoted mothers, stern fathers, and obedient children, because, out of hatred for their own devotion, sternness, and obedience, they'd be only too happy to turn us over to the aforementioned institutions. We'll distrust those doctors who busy themselves with mental health. They would try to convince us that we're sick. And poets. They would want to make us believe in tragedy. Yes, we'll distrust poets, priests, and doctors, because if we reject sickness, tragedy, and sin they'll call the police. To repeat: If we stay away from doctors, poets, judges, legislators, the clergy, mothers, fathers, and children, not to mention divine, human, and natural morality, nothing can happen to us. We'll be happy! (*She exits left.*)

SCENE 57

Enter right VATZLAV *with his litter. He looks around, cups his ear, and listens intently. He puts the litter down, climbs up on the chair, looks around, and listens again.*

VATZLAV: I don't hear them any more. Where are they? I don't get it. What's going to happen now? Yes, they took a few chunks out of me, but at least they protected me against the thieves, peddlers, and agitators who are always trying to make off with what you've earned by your honest work. I'd rather be bitten now and then than go without their protection. Yes, little puppies, where are you? If it weren't for you, wild boars, raccoons, and all sorts of forest riffraff would multiply like rabbits. Maybe they won't be gone for long. Let's not give up hope. But in the meantime, let's try to find a safe place for our property. (*He loads the litter on his back and exits left.*)

SCENE 58

Enter right BOBBIE *and* MR. BAT. *They are still fighting, but now it is* MR. BAT *who retreats. They exist left, fighting.*

SCENE 59

Enter right THE LACKEY, *running with a limp. His face is black, his clothes are torn.*

THE LACKEY: Master, oh, master . . . (*He exits left.*)

SCENE 60

Enter right QUAIL *and* SASSAFRAS *carrying bundles containing all of their worldly possessions.*

SASSAFRAS: All this on account of your cold.
QUAIL: I'm feeling better now.
SASSAFRAS: Sure, now that my house has burned down.
QUAIL: Mine's burned down, too. Fire's bad.

SASSAFRAS: Yeah, fire's bad, but it's nothing like a good flood.

QUAIL: Or hail.

SASSAFRAS: What do you think of the plague?

QUAIL: You're so picky and choosy. I take what I get.

SASSAFRAS: 'Cause you're ignorant.

They exit left.

SCENE 61

Enter right MR. BAT *and* BOBBIE *fighting fiercely.* BOBBIE *retreats. They exit left, fighting.*

SCENE 62

Enter right THE LACKEY, *staggering. He crosses the stage slowly, falls, crawls a few feet, stops, and dies. Enter right two* SOLDIERS *and* THE OFFICER. *They wear helmets with wide rims, coats of mail, tight-fitting breeches. The* SOLDIERS *carry lances,* THE OFFICER *carries a sword.*

THE OFFICER: Remove this body.

The SOLDIERS *carry* THE LACKEY *out left,* THE OFFICER *follows.*

SCENE 63

VATZLAV'S VOICE (*off stage*): Fire! Fire! Help! Help!
VATZLAV (*he enters right, dragging his litter*): Oh, my years
  of bitter toil . . . Oh, my property! (*He takes off his
  hat and beats the chair as though to put out a fire.*)

SCENE 64

Enter right GENERAL BARBARO *in helmet, golden coat of
mail, wielding a sword. Behind him a* SOLDIER *carrying the
mummified* GENIUS *at the end of his pole.* THE GENIUS *points
the way with one finger of his upraised hand, his face is
waxen, two red circles adorn his cheeks, his lips are heavily
rouged, around his neck hangs a wreath of paper roses. A
gold halo shines above his head.* DRUMMERS *and* LANCERS
follow behind him. The troop stops. VATZLAV *puts on his
hat and hides under his litter.*

GENERAL BARBARO: That does it, men. The war's over. I
  always said these degenerates would be a pushover.

SCENE 65

Enter left QUAIL *and* SASSAFRAS *escorted by* SOLDIERS *who prod them in their backs with lances.*

SASSAFRAS: How's it going, neighbor Quail?

QUAIL: I've got shooting pains in my back.

SASSAFRAS: I've been having little twinges myself.

QUAIL: We must have caught cold.

GENERAL BARBARO: Who are you?

QUAIL: I'm Quail. This is Sassafras.

GENERAL BARBARO: I didn't ask for your names. Are you rich or poor?

QUAIL: We're poor, boss.

GENERAL BARBARO: Lucky for you. We have come to liberate you. To help the poor, destroy the rich, as our beloved leader has taught us. (*He bows low to the mummy.*) May he live forever!

He raises his hand as if to strike the SOLDIER *holding the mummy.*

Is that a way to hold him?

Frightened, the SOLDIER *raises the pole higher.*

That's it. (*To* QUAIL *and* SASSAFRAS.) Well, what do you think of him?

QUAIL: Pretty.

SASSAFRAS: But kind of stiff.

GENERAL BARBARO: I beg your pardon?

SASSAFRAS: Kind of lifeless.

GENERAL BARBARO (*putting his sword to Sassafras's throat*):
I didn't quite get that.

SASSAFRAS: Lively, that's the word. Bless my soul, I never
saw anyone looking so lively.

QUAIL: In the pink.

GENERAL BARBARO (*lowering his sword*): That's better. (*He
picks his ear with his finger.*) Sometimes I'm deaf in
my left ear . . . He's lively, all right, and what's more,
he's alive. We've just embalmed him a little to keep
him from spoiling. The surface may be a bit shiny but
it keeps out the rain. In all other respects he's in good
health, better than you . . . And smart! He knows
everything. (*To the* SOLDIER.) Higher, you jackass!

SCENE 66

Enter left MR. BAT, *unarmed, escorted by a* SOLDIER.

GENERAL BARBARO: Who's this?

SOLDIER: Mr. Bat, the capitalist. He sucked the blood of the
people.

GENERAL BARBARO (*to* QUAIL *and* SASSAFRAS): Is that true?

QUAIL: Yes, sir, he sure did.

SASSAFRAS: An all-day sucker, that's what he was.

GENERAL BARBARO: Hang him.

SASSAFRAS: Long live!

GENERAL BARBARO: The capitalist?

QUAIL: Of course not, boss. He meant the hangman.

GENERAL BARBARO: Oh, that's different.

QUAIL: He knows the score. Don't you, Sassafras?

SASSAFRAS: Sure thing. No use long-living a man with a rope around his neck.

GENERAL BARBARO: Hmm, you seem to have a head on your shoulders.

SASSAFRAS: That's right, boss. We're the people. That's the wisdom of the people.

QUAIL: Comes with our mother's milk, boss.

GENERAL BARBARO: Go in peace. And never forget that you've been liberated by the liberators.

QUAIL (*bowing*): Thanks, boss.

SASSAFRAS (*bowing*): Thank you kindly, boss.

GENERAL BARBARO (*to a* SOLDIER): Take this man to the gallows.

SOLDIER *exits with* MR. BAT.

QUAIL (*aside to* SASSAFRAS): Let's get out of here, Sassafras. From now on we'll just have to suck our own blood.

SASSAFRAS: Got to keep up with the times.

QUAIL *and* SASSAFRAS *exit left.*

SCENE 67

GENERAL BARBARO (*to* SOLDIERS *who brought in* QUAIL *and* SASSAFRAS): Hang those fellows, too . . .

SOLDIERS *make a move to leave.*

But cut the rope. That'll teach them gratitude. First you hang them, then you cut the rope. They're too smart. That'll take them down a peg.

SOLDIERS *exit left.*

SCENE 68

Enter left two SOLDIERS *escorting* BOBBIE *who wears his bear mask but is no longer armed.*

GENERAL BARBARO: Who are you?

BOBBIE: The bear.

GENERAL BARBARO: I say you're a camel.

BOBBIE: Have I got a hump?

GENERAL BARBARO: How do I know? Maybe you haven't. And maybe you have. If you have, you must be hiding it, because I don't see it. In that case you're circumventing the authorities. And if you haven't got a hump . . . how do I know you wouldn't have hidden it if you had one? In either case, you're guilty because now everybody's circumventing the authorities—or trying to. So to be on the safe side, we'll put you down as a camel.

BOBBIE: I am a wild, free, and independent bear, and I recognize no authority.

GENERAL BARBARO: That proves you're a camel.

BOBBIE: I serve no man.

GENERAL BARBARO: A camel if ever there was one.

BOBBIE: Down with authority.

GENERAL BARBARO: Definitely a camel! (*To the* SOLDIERS.) Cut off his camelhood. This camel's voice is too deep.

Two SOLDIERS *lead* BOBBIE *out left.*

SCENE 69

Enter left OEDIPUS *led by two* SOLDIERS.

OEDIPUS: I wish to register a complaint.

GENERAL BARBARO: Go ahead, old man, I like denunciations.

OEDIPUS: A young man wants to kill his father and violate his mother.

GENERAL BARBARO: Must be full of beans.

OEDIPUS: Which is contrary to divine, human, and natural law.

GENERAL BARBARO: Wait a minute. Who are you?

OEDIPUS: I am the exemplar of divine, human, and natural law.

GENERAL BARBARO: That's quite a mouthful. (*He makes himself comfortable in the chair under which* VATZLAV *is hiding.*) Hmm . . . You must be a VIP.

OEDIPUS: Yes, indeed. An indispensable model for all mankind.

GENERAL BARBARO: An official personage, so to speak . . .

OEDIPUS: Upon my shoulders rests the order of the world.

GENERAL BARBARO: Are you as important as a king?

OEDIPUS: I was a king but I renounced my kingdom to become the guardian of the law. It follows that my office is the highest of all human dignities.

GENERAL BARBARO (*leaning back in the chair*): You mean you're more important than me? Holier than our beloved leader?

OEDIPUS: No one is holier than I.

GENERAL BARBARO (*to the* SOLDIERS): Boys, take care of this senior citizen. Teach him the realities of life . . . Let's go, boys, I want to see teamwork!

OEDIPUS: What does this mean?

GENERAL BARBARO: It means they're going to screw you.

OEDIPUS: I am Oedipus Rex!

GENERAL BARBARO: We don't care if you're Santa Claus. With God's help we've fucked better people than you. Haven't we, boys?

SOLDIERS: Hooray!

GENERAL BARBARO: See? Don't worry. They'll fix you up.

OEDIPUS: Violate me? Me? An old man?

GENERAL BARBARO: That's the way it is, chum.

OEDIPUS: Will the heavens not take pity? Will the sun not go out and darkness fall upon the earth? . . . Between you and me, what pleasure . . .

GENERAL BARBARO: Who said anything about pleasure? Take a look at yourself. We're doing it for the glory of the flag and to demonstrate our virility which shrinks from nothing, not even from you. We fear no sacrifice. We'll screw you with tears in our eyes, but we'll screw you. Right, boys?

SOLDIERS: Hooray!

OEDIPUS: Why this sacrifice?

GENERAL BARBARO: To humble your pride. (*He stands up.*) So you were a king? An exemplar? A VIP? Good. I'm glad you're not some poor bastard. A venerable patriarch? That's perfect. Today my soldiers are going to screw you. A hero of art and culture? They'll screw the culture and art out of you. A guardian of the law? The conscience of mankind? A good stiff cock up your ass will knock that out of you. Show you who's running things around here. (*He sits down.*) Okay, boys, take him away.

OEDIPUS: Woe is me!

> *Drums. Two* SOLDIERS *grab* OEDIPUS *under the arms and drag him out left. The entire troop follows them as the drums roll and the procession ends with the bearer of the mummy.* GENERAL BARBARO, *seated in Vatzlav's litter, stretches, yawns, and falls asleep without dropping his unsheathed sword.*

SCENE 70

> VATZLAV *issues cautiously from his hiding place under the chair. He looks around, on all sides. He stops in front of the sleeping* GENERAL BARBARO.

VATZLAV: He's asleep. Made himself comfortable . . . In my chair. I bet he feels pretty good. I wonder what he's dreaming about. Before he took my place he could dream about taking it. What can he dream about now? About losing it? Conclusion: He had pleasanter dreams before. I could feel sorry for him except that he's having his bad dreams sitting down while I'm making a good speech standing up.

> GENERAL BARBARO *moves restlessly in his sleep and sighs.*

All right, sigh. Your conscience must be torturing you for taking my chair. A nightmare. It must be killing you. I'd give it a hand, except you might wake up, the nightmare would vanish, and I'd be left holding the bag. But the more I look at your crooked mug, the more I want to fix it for you. I'd better look at something else. Another minute and I won't be able to resist. (*He turns his head, then looks at* GENERAL BARBARO, *then looks away again.*) No, a little patience. (*He looks again.*) I can feel myself slipping. (*He turns his head.*) Don't look . . . Don't look . . . (*He looks.*) Or I'll bash his head in . . . (*He turns away and covers his eyes with his hands.*) Don't look . . . Don't look . . .

VATZLAV *looks and raises his hand as if to strike.* GENERAL BARBARO *shifts his position. Frightened,* VATZLAV *jumps back.* GENERAL BARBARO *continues sleeping.*

Whew! Narrow escape I had there. Oh, well, maybe it's good he's asleep. He's not nice when he's awake. I'll let him sleep, just take back my property. But how? First I'll disarm him, then we'll see.

He touches General Barbaro's hand and tries to take the sword. GENERAL BARBARO *grunts in his sleep.* VATZLAV *jumps back.*

All right, all right. I'm not interested in your property. Just return mine and we'll call it square. Nothing to get sore about. Come on . . . Hell, he won't listen to reason.

He takes GENERAL BARBARO *by one leg and tries to pull him off the chair. Each time* GENERAL BARBARO *moves or grunts,* VATZLAV *stops, puts a finger to his lips, and tries to soothe him as if he were a child having bad dreams. Finally, half off the chair,* GENERAL BARBARO *moves so violently that* VATZLAV *gives up.*

Is he stubborn! Oh, no, my fine-feathered friend, don't think you can get rid of me so easily. Hanging people,

cutting things off people, okay, that's your business.
But my property is my property. Give it back!

VATZLAV *approaches the chair from behind, seizes the*
ends of the poles, raises the litter with GENERAL BAR-
BARO *in it and drags it to the right like a wheelbarrow.*
GENERAL BARBARO *slips to the ground. Suddenly* GEN-
ERAL BARBARO *jumps up with his feet together and*
immediately assumes a fencer's stance. But he doesn't
know where his adversary is and does not see VATZLAV.

GENERAL BARBARO: Ho, guards!

Three SOLDIERS *run in, two from the left, one from the*
right, with lances lowered. They surround VATZLAV,
touching him with their lances. VATZLAV *raises his*
hands. GENERAL BARBARO *approaches him and examines*
him attentively.

Are you one of us?

VATZLAV *shakes his head.*

Where do you belong?

VATZLAV: I'm a foreigner.

GENERAL BARBARO: He's too thin to be from here, but too
fat to be one of us. With the new regime, of course,
the natives will get thin and we'll get fat, but then he'll
be too fat for a native and too thin for one of us. I'd
better hold him until tomorrow. If by then he hasn't
definitely gained or lost weight, we'll hand him over to
the executioner. Because a man has got to belong
somewhere.

He sits down in the litter. Two SOLDIERS *pick it up. To*
avoid being encumbered by their lances, they pass them
along the poles of the litter or sling them over their

backs. *They exit left, carrying* GENERAL BARBARO. VATZ-
LAV *follows, escorted by the third* SOLDIER.

SCENE 71

Enter right QUAIL *and* SASSAFRAS, *each with a rope around
his neck. The ropes are of equal length and trail on the
ground.*

SASSAFRAS: All this talk about equality. And now your rope
is longer than mine.
QUAIL: That's impossible.
SASSAFRAS: Why is it impossible?
QUAIL: Because yours is longer than mine.
SASSAFRAS: I'd give you the shirt off my back, but if they
hang us equal they should cut us down equal. It ain't
right your having more rope.
QUAIL: I don't know about that. What bugs me is having
less.
SASSAFRAS: Give back the difference.
QUAIL: You give back the difference.
SASSAFRAS: If that's the way it is, if you won't do what's
right, I'll complain to our liberator. Good man, he'll
string us up equally.
QUAIL: Good idea. He'll cut your rope down to size.
SASSAFRAS: He won't let me get the short end.
QUAIL *and* SASSAFRAS (*in unison*): He will do justice.

They exit left.

SCENE 72

Enter right VATZLAV. *He is dressed in the shirt and tattered pants which he wore in Scene 1. He has neither his blazer nor bowler nor watch nor ring, but he still has his clogs. He is followed by* THE EXECUTIONER *in red tights, his face covered by a red hood, carrying a large double-edged sword pointed upwards.*

VATZLAV: Somebody hasn't kept his word in this deal. It could be Providence or it could be me. No, come to think of it, that's not it. We made a pact. We both did what we were supposed to, and nothing came of it. I wanted to be free, rich, happy, and I haven't really succeeded, though no one could deny I've had my freedom, that I've had money off and on, and been happy from time to time. So I can't find fault with Providence, but I've nothing much to thank it for, either. I've been free as often as not, glutted as often as hungry, happy as often as sad. For a time I was young and now I'm old. I've gone in and out of the house an equal number of times. I've been awake and I've slept, done a certain amount of loving and a certain amount of hating. All in all, it's time to break up my partnership with Providence because it hasn't done either of us any good, and retire from business because the debit cancels out the credit. Altogether, living is an ungrateful profession. And now they want me to be a professional corpse. But taken as a profession,

death is just as stupid as life. What I'd like is amateur
status. I wouldn't mind dying now and then, any more
than I'd mind living. What I object to is sinking my
whole capital into either one of them. These new
bosses seem to attach a great deal of importance to my
execution. They're determined to have me for a part-
ner. But dying to order doesn't appeal to me . . . it
would tie me up for all eternity. So I'll turn down
their offer and clear out of this shop where I don't want
to buy anything and have nothing to sell.

*He takes out a cardboard jumping jack, pulls the string
and the jumping jack moves. He shows it to* THE EXE-
CUTIONER *who looks at the toy with interest and laughs
good-naturedly. He holds out his hand and* VATZLAV
gives him the jumping jack. THE EXECUTIONER *holds it
by the top string because the sword in his other hand
prevents him from correctly operating the toy. Eager
to oblige,* VATZLAV *helps him, the jumping jack moves,*
THE EXECUTIONER *laughs. He gives* VATZLAV *his sword
and operates the jumping jack with both hands.* VATZ-
LAV *sneaks off to the right, turns, and then runs out.*
THE EXECUTIONER *continues playing with the jumping
jack but suddenly stops and realizes that his victim
is gone. He stops laughing. With an inarticulate shout
of rage, he dashes off in pursuit of* VATZLAV.

SCENE 73

Enter right MRS. BAT *in deep mourning. She leads* BOBBIE,
*in his bear costume, by the hand. Little red bows and silver
bells are attached to his hands and feet.* MRS. BAT *beats*

time on a tambourine as BOBBIE *performs an awkward bear dance.* VATZLAV *runs in from the left with the sword over his shoulder.*

MRS. BAT (*holding out the tambourine to* VATZLAV): Alms for the poor bear and his keeper!

> VATZLAV *stops, digs into his pockets, and tosses a coin into the tambourine before running out right.* MRS. BAT *moves left, shaking the tambourine as* BOBBIE *dances beside her. Enter left* THE EXECUTIONER *holding a noose.*

Alms for the poor bear . . .

> *Paying no attention,* THE EXECUTIONER *runs out right. After a moment,* MRS. BAT *and* BOBBIE *exit left.*

SCENE 74

Enter right SASSAFRAS *and* QUAIL *with their ropes around their necks.* VATZLAV *runs in from the left with the sword over his shoulder.*

QUAIL: Hey, boss.
SASSAFRAS: Wait, boss.

> VATZLAV *stops running.*

QUAIL: Settle our argument.
SASSAFRAS: Who's got the longer rope?
QUAIL: Him!
SASSAFRAS: Him!

VATZLAV: Since you both think the other's rope is longer, swap ropes and don't bother me. I'm in a hurry. If I waste time on your ropes I'll get one all my own and I won't even have time to see if it's longer than yours.

SASSAFRAS: What's that? Longer?

QUAIL: Longer than ours?

SASSAFRAS: Oh no, you don't.

QUAIL: Get him, neighbor.

They pounce on VATZLAV, *throw his sword to the ground, and beat him.* THE EXECUTIONER *enters left with his noose.* VATZLAV *tears himself away from the peasants and runs out right with* THE EXECUTIONER *hard on his heels.* QUAIL *and* SASSAFRAS *exit left, shaking their fists at* VATZLAV.

SCENE 75

Enter left VATZLAV *breathing heavily; his hand is on his heart.*

VATZLAV: Whew! I've shaken him off. That's not surprising . . . I've had more training running away than he has. High time. I can't go another step. When I think of all the running away I've done in my life! But this time my training won't help me because here I am back on the beach. The waves dash against the shore, the gulls cry, not a ship in sight. But what good is all this empty space if I can't go on? (*He sits down facing the sea upstage. He places his hands over his eyes and views the horizon.*)

SCENE 76

A woman is heard moaning and weeping to the left. Enter
JUSTINE. *She has lost her wreath, her hair is in disarray, her*
dress is dirty and torn. She carries a baby. She moves right.

VATZLAV: Hey!

> JUSTINE *stops, turns towards him and stops crying.*

Say, I know you. Aren't you the daughter of that old
codger who invented justice?

JUSTINE: No.

VATZLAV: What do you mean, no? He gave you the name
of justice and made you exhibit yourself in public. I
made a pile of money on it.

JUSTINE: It wasn't me.

VATZLAV: Maybe not. You didn't have a baby then. (*He*
approaches her but she looks away.) Let's see. Don't
be ashamed. Hm . . . he reminds me of somebody,
too. Who's the happy father?

JUSTINE: The father is happy, the mother is miserable.

VATZLAV: Really? Why?

JUSTINE: I don't want to be a mother.

VATZLAV: Then how come . . .

JUSTINE: I didn't know where babies came from.

VATZLAV: Where did you think they came from?

JUSTINE: The head.

VATZLAV: The head?

JUSTINE: By the workings of reason.

VATZLAV (*aside*): The poor girl is off her rocker.

JUSTINE: Daddy told me to watch the birds and the flowers
. . . "It's the same with them . . . Nature is reasonable . . . I begot you with my head and bore you
with my head . . ." I was going to be a queen. (*She
weeps.*)

VATZLAV: Come on, take it easy . . . (*Aside.*) That's it,
she's cracked.

JUSTINE (*weeping*): The world is reasonable . . .

VATZLAV: Reasonable? The world?

JUSTINE: That's what I thought . . . (*She weeps.*)

VATZLAV: Poor thing . . . Where are you going with the
fruit of your father's wisdom?

JUSTINE: To see the little fishies.

VATZLAV: You're going to drown it?

JUSTINE: The little fishies are reasonable, too. They won't
do her any harm.

VATZLAV: Give the bastard to me!

He grabs the baby as JUSTINE *moves away.*

Hey! Where are you going?

JUSTINE: I'm going to tell the little birdies my troubles.
(*She runs out left.*)

SCENE 77

VATZLAV: Birdies and fishies! . . . What am I going to do
with this brat? I've got nothing for her to eat. And,
besides, I hate kids. (*A police whistle is heard on the
left.*) Maybe I could tell them I'm a nursing mother?

92 • **Slawomir Mrozek**

The benefits of progress, I'll tell them. See, I've had a baby. Why wouldn't they believe me since they believe in progress, reason, and justice? Except that they'll kill me, kid and all. (*He goes upstage, stops, faces the sea, and addresses the baby.*) See the other shore? . . . Neither do I. But if we could get there you might grow up to be somebody. Not here. (*A second blast from the police whistle.*) I've heard that a whole people passed through the sea and reached the other shore without getting wet. (*A third blast of the police whistle. Holding the baby in one arm, he takes off his shoes and rolls up his trousers. He picks up his shoes and walks to the far end of the platform with the motions of a man entering the water.*) Brr . . . it's cold . . . (*He stops. Visible from the waist up, he turns to the audience.*) You wait here. If I don't come back, you'll know I've made it. Then you can follow. (*He slowly disappears behind the stage.*)